Stories of the Quran

Isma'il bin 'Umar bin Kathir al-Qurashi Al-Damishqi

Copyright ©

TX0008972332-TX0008431188

King Fahd Complex for Printing

Editor: Noah Ibn Kathir - Al-Imam Ahmad

Dua [1] for starting salah (prayer):

سُبْحَانَكَ اللَّهُمَّ وَبِحَمْدِكَ وَتَبَارَكَ اسْمُكَ

Glory and praise be to You, O Allah. Blessed be Your name

وَتَعَالَى جَدُّكَ وَلاَ إِلَهَ غَيْرُكَ

and exalted be Your majesty,
there is none worthy of worship except You

When the Messenger of Allah (saw) started to pray, he would say:
'Glory and praise be to You, O Allah. Blessed be Your name and exalted be Your majesty, there is none worthy of worship except You.'

Invocation during Sujood/Prostration and Ruku [2]:

سُبْحَانَكَ اللَّهُمَّ رَبَّنَا وَبِحَمْدِكَ اللَّهُمَّ اغْفِرْ لِي

Glory is to You, O Allah, our Lord, and praise is Yours.
O Allah, forgive me.

'Aishah (May Allah be pleased with her) reported:
The Prophet (saw) used to recite frequently in his bowing and prostration:
"Subhanak- Allahumma, Rabbana wa bihamdika. Allahum-maghfir li."
[Al-Bukhari and Muslim]

It was narrated from Ali, that:
When the Messenger of Allah started to pray, he would say Takbir, then say:

Dua 3 for starting salah (prayer)

وَجَّهْتُ وَجْهِيَ لِلَّذِي فَطَرَ السَّمَوَاتِ وَالأَرْضَ حَنِيفًا

Verily, I have turned my face toward Him
who created the Heavens and the Earth, worhsipping none but Allah alone,

وَمَا أَنَا مِنَ الْمُشْرِكِينَ إِنَّ صَلاَتِي وَنُسُكِي وَمَحْيَايَ وَمَمَاتِي

and I am not of the idolaters. Verily, my prayer, my sacrifice, my living, and my dying

لِلَّهِ رَبِّ الْعَالَمِينَ لاَ شَرِيكَ لَهُ وَبِذَلِكَ أُمِرْتُ وَأَنَا مِنَ الْمُسْلِمِينَ

are for Allah, the Lord of the all that exists. He has no partner.
And of this I have been commanded, and I am one of the Muslims.

Biography of Hafiz Ibn Kathir
Author of Tafsir Ibn Kathir

He is a very respected Imam, Abu Al-Fida', `Imad Ad-Din Isma il bin 'Umar bin Kathir Al-Qurashi Al-Busrawi - Busraian in origin; Dimashqi in training, learning and residence.

Ibn Kathir was born in the city of Busra in 701 H. His father was the Friday speaker of the village, but he died while Ibn Kathir was only 4 years old. Ibn Kathir's brother, Shaykh Abdul-Wahhab, reared him and taught him until he moved to Damascus in 706 H., when he was five years old.

Ibn Kathir's Teachers

Ibn Kathir studied Fiqh - Islamic jurisprudence - with Burhan Ad-Din, Ibrahim bin `Abdur-Rahman Al-Fizari, known as Ibn Al-Firkah (who died in 729 H). Ibn Kathir heard Hadiths from `Isa bin Al-Mutim, Ahmad bin Abi Talib, (Ibn Ash-Shahnah) (who died in 730 H).

Ibn Al-Hajjar, (who died in 730 H), and the Hadith narrator of Ash-Sham (modern day Syria and surrounding areas); Baha Ad-Din Al-Qasim bin Muzaffar bin `Asakir (who died in 723 H), and Ibn Ash-Shirdzi, Ishaq bin Yahya Al-Ammuddi, also known as `Afif Ad-Din, the Zahiriyyah Shaykh who died in 725 H, and Muhammad bin Zarrad. He remained with Jamal Ad-Din, Yusuf bin Az-Zaki AlMizzi who died in 724 H, he benefited from his knowledge and also married his daughter. He also read with Shaykh Al-Islam, Taqi Ad-Din Ahmad bin `Abdul-Halim bin `Abdus-Salam bin Taymiyyah who died in 728 H. He also read with the Imam Hafiz and historian Shams Ad-Din, Muhammad bin Ahmad bin Uthman bin Qaymaz Adh-Dhahabi, who died in 748 H. Also, Abu Musa Al-Qarafai, Abu Al-Fath Ad-Dabbusi and 'Ali bin `Umar As-Suwani and others who gave him permission to transmit the knowledge he learned with them in Egypt.

In his book, Al-Mu jam Al-Mukhtas, Al-Hafiz Adh-Dhaliabi wrote that Ibn Kathir was, "The Imam, scholar of jurisprudence, skillful scholar of Hadith, renowned Fagih and scholar of Tafsir who wrote several beneficial books."

Further, in Ad-Durar Al-Kdminah, Al-Hafiz Ibn Hajar AlAsqalani said, "Ibn Kathir worked on the subject of the Hadith in the areas of texts and chains of narrators. He had a good memory, his books became popular during his lifetime, and people benefited from them after his death."

Also, the renowned historian Abu Al-Mahasin, Jamal Ad-Din Yusuf bin Sayf Ad-Din (Ibn Taghri Bardi), said in his book, AlManhal As-Safi, "He is the Shaykh, the Imam, the great scholar `Imad Ad-Din Abu Al-Fida'. He learned extensively and was very active in collecting knowledge and writing. He was excellent in the areas of Fiqh, Tafsfr and Hadith. He collected knowledge, authored (books), taught, narrated Hadith and wrote. He had immense knowledge in the fields of Hadith, Tafsir, Fiqh, the Arabic language, and so forth. He gave Fatawa (religious verdicts) and taught until he died, may Allah grant him mercy. He was known for his precision and vast knowledge, and as a scholar of history, Hadith and Tafsir."

Ibn Kathir's Students

Ibn Hajji was one of Ibn Kathir's students, and he described Ibn Kathir: "He had the best memory of the Hadith texts. He also had the most knowledge concerning the narrators and authenticity, his contemporaries and teachers admitted to these qualities. Every time I met him I gained some benefit from him."

Also, Ibn Al-`Imad Al-Hanbali said in his book, Shadhardt Adh-Dhahab, "He is the renowned Hafiz `Imad Ad-Din, whose memory was excellent, whose forgetfulness was miniscule, whose understanding was adequate, and who had good knowledge in the Arabic language." Also, Ibn Habib said about Ibn Kathir, "He heard knowledge and collected it and wrote various books. He brought comfort to the ears with his Fatwas and narrated Hadith and brought benefit to other people. The papers that contained his Fatwas were transmitted to the various (Islamic) provinces. Further, he was known for his precision and encompassing knowledge."

Ibn Kathir's Books

1 - One of the greatest books that Ibn Kathir wrote was his Tafsir of the Noble Qur'an, which is one of the best Tafsir that rely on narrations [of Ahadith, the Tafsir of the Companions, etc.]. The Tafsir by Ibn Kathir was printed many times and several scholars have summarized it.

2- The History Collection known as Al-Biddyah, which was printed in 14 volumes under the name Al-Bidayah wanNihdyah, and contained the stories of the Prophets and previous nations, the Prophet's Seerah (life story) and Islamic history until his time. He also added a book Al-Fitan, about the Signs of the Last Hour.

3- At-Takmil ft Ma`rifat Ath-Thiqatwa Ad-Du'afa walMajdhil which Ibn Kathir collected from the books of his two Shaykhs Al-Mizzi and Adh-Dhahabi; Al-Kdmal and Mizan Al-Ftiddl. He added several benefits regarding the subject of Al-Jarh and AtT'adil.

4- Al-Hadi was-Sunan ft Ahadith Al-Masdnfd was-Sunan which is also known by, Jami` Al-Masdnfd. In this book, Ibn Kathir collected the narrations of Imams Ahmad bin Hanbal, Al-Bazzar, Abu Ya`la Al-Mawsili, Ibn Abi Shaybah and from the six collections of Hadith: the Two Sahihs [Al-Bukhari and Muslim] and the Four Sunan

[Abu Dawud, At-Tirmidhi, AnNasa and Ibn Majah]. Ibn Kathir divided this book according to areas of Fiqh.

5-Tabaqat Ash-Shafiyah which also contains the virtues of Imam Ash-Shafi.

6- Ibn Kathir wrote references for the Ahadith of Adillat AtTanbfh, from the Shafi school of Fiqh.

7- Ibn Kathir began an explanation of Sahih Al-Bukhari, but he did not finish it.

8- He started writing a large volume on the Ahkam (Laws), but finished only up to the Hajj rituals.

9- He summarized Al-Bayhaqi's 'Al-Madkhal. Many of these books were not printed.

10- He summarized `Ulum Al-Hadith, by Abu `Amr bin AsSalah and called it Mukhtasar `Ulum Al-Hadith. Shaykh Ahmad Shakir, the Egyptian Muhaddith, printed this book along with his commentary on it and called it Al-Ba'th Al-Hathfth fi Sharh Mukhtasar `Ulum Al-Hadith.

11- As-Sfrah An-Nabawiyyah, which is contained in his book Al-Biddyah, and both of these books are in print.

12- A research on Jihad called Al-Ijtihad ft Talabi Al-Jihad, which was printed several times.

Ibn Kathir's Death

Al-Hafiz Ibn Hajar Al-Asgalani said, "Ibn Kathir lost his sight just before his life ended. He died in Damascus in 774 H." May Allah grant mercy upon Ibn Kathir and make him among the residents of His Paradise.

Table of Contents

1. The Story of Qabil and Habil and Qabil (Cain and Abel)
2. The Story of Marut and Harut
3. The Story of Dwellers of the Town
4. The Story of the Heifer
5. The Story of Prophet Moses and Al-Khadir
6. The Story of Qarun
7. The Story of Bilqis (Queen of Sheba)
8. The Story of Saba (Sheba)
9. The Story of Uzair (Ezra)
10. The Story of Dhul Qarnain
11. The Story of Magog and Gog
12. The Story of People of the Cave
13. The Story of the Believer and the Disbeliever
14. The Story of People of the Garden
15. The Story of the Sabbath-Breakers
16. The Story of Luqman
17. The Story of People of the Ditch
18. The Story of Barsisa the Worshipper (The Renegade)
19. The Story of Yemen and Owners of the Elephant

The Story of Habil and Qabil "Able and Cain" (1)
The First Crime on Earth

Allah the Almighty said:

"And (O'Muhammad (peace and blessing be upon him) recite to them (to the Jewish people) the story of the two sons of Adam (Qabil and Habil) in truth; when each offered a sacrifice (to Allah), it was accepted from the one but not from the other. The latter said to the former: "I will surely kill you." The former said: "Verily, Allah accepts only from those who are Al-Muttaqun (the pious)." "If you do stretch your hand against me to kill me, I shall never stretch my hand against you to kill you: for I fear Allah, the Lord of the Alamin (mankind, jinn, and all that exists)."

"Verily, I intend to let you draw my sin on yourself as well as yours, then you will be one of the dwellers of the Fire; and that is the recompense of the Zalimin (polytheists and wrong-doers);" So the Nafs (self) of the other (latter one) encouraged him and made fair-seeming to him the murder of his brother; he murdered him and became one of the losers; Then Allah sent a crow who scratched the ground to show him to hide the dead body of his brother; He (the murderer) said: "Woe to me! Am I not even able to be as this crow and to hide the dead body of my brother? Then he became one of those who regretted". (Al-Maidah, 27-31)

Adam (Peace be upon him) used to get the male brought by one birth married to the female brought by the other. Hence, it was supposed that Abel would get married to Cain's sister who was better and more beautiful than anyone else. At the same time, Cain wanted to keep her for himself. Adam (Peace be upon him) ordered him to allow Abefl to marry her, but he totally refused.

Then, Adam (Peace be upon him) ordered both (Cain and Abel) to offer a sacrifice to Allah Almighty. Adam (peace be upon him) then set forth towards Mecca to perform Pilgrimage. Just before leaving, Adam tried to entrust (the affairs of) his children to the heavens, the earth and finally to the mountains, but all declined to shoulder the (heavy) trust. Thereupon, Cain accepted the trust and after

Adam went away they (Cain and Abel) offered their sacrifices to Allah. Abel offered a fat she-goat, while Cain offered a bundle of bad plants. Later, a fire came down from heaven and consumed the sacrifice offered by Abel and left untouched that of Cain. Cain became livid with rage and said to his brother: I will kill you so as not to marry my sister, Abel said: "Verily, Allah accepts only from those who are Al-Muttaqun (the pious people)."

The murdered (Abel) was stronger (than the murderer, Cain), but he refused to stretch his hand against his brother to kill him due to his piety and God-fearing.

Adam (Peace be upon him) was present there when they offered their sacrifices. After Abel's sacrifice was accepted, Cain said to his father, Adam: "It was accepted only from him because you invoked Allah for his sake." And, he secretly intended something against his brother. One day, Abel was late and Adam sent Cain to look for him. The two brothers met and Cain said: "Your sacrifice was accepted and mine was not." Abel said: "Verily, Allah accepts only from those who are Al-Muttaqun (the pious)." Cain got angry and hit his brother with an iron rod and Abel fell dead at once.

It was said that Cain killed Abel by throwing a rock on his head while he was asleep.

It was also said: Cain choked Abel violently and bit him to death as beasts do. However, Abel's saying when Cain threatened to kill him: "If you do stretch your hand against me to kill me, I shall never stretch my hand against you to kill you: for I fear Allah."

The Messenger of Allah (Peace be upon him) said: "When two Muslims confront each other and the one amongst them attacks his brother with a weapon, both of them get into Hell- Fire."

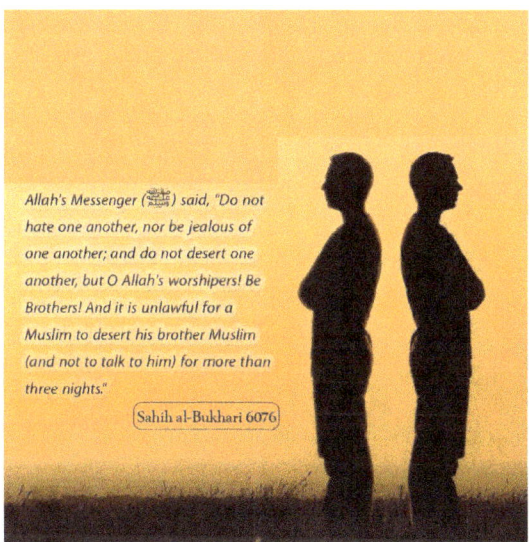

Allah the Almighty said: "Verily, I intend to let you draw my sin (on yourself) as well as yours, then you will be one of the people of the Fire."

The Messenger of Allah (peace and blessings be upon him) said: "There will be a period of turmoil in which the one who sits will be better than one who stands and the one who stands will be better than one who walks and the one who walks will be better than one who runs." Someone said: "What is your opinion if someone entered my home and stretched his hand to kill me?" The Prophet (Peace be upon him) said: "Be just like the son of Adam (Abel)."

The Messenger of Allah (Peace be upon him) said: "None (no human being) is killed or murdered (unjustly), but a part of responsibility for the crime is laid on the first son of Adam who invented the tradition of killing (murdering on earth)."

There is a cave, called the "Blood Cave", in a mountain in the northern part of Syria. It is thought to be the scene of the crime where Cain killed his brother Abel. The people living there came to know this through the People of the Book (Christians and Jews) and only Allah Almighty knows the truth.

Allah Almighty said: "Then, Allah sent a crow who scratched the ground to show him how to hide the dead body of his brother. He (the murderer) said: 'Woe to me! Am I not even able to be as this crow and to hide the dead body of my brother?'"

Cain carried his brother on his back for a full year (not knowing what to do with his brother's corpse!). Others said: He carried him on his back for one hundred years till Allah sent two crows who fought against one another. One of them was killed. The murderer scratched the ground to hide the body of the dead crow. Seeing him doing that, Cain said: Woe to me! Am I not even able to do as this crow and to hide the dead body of my brother? Then, he buried the body of his dead brother and covered it with earth.

Adam became very ill at heart and felt great sorrow for his dead son, Abel. Cain was brought punishment very soon afterwards. On the same day he killed his brother, Abel, his foot was tied up to his thighbone and his face was forcibly directed up to the sun disk. His face used to go where the sun goes as a way of punishment and penalty in return for what he had done to his own brother.

The Messenger of Allah (Peace be upon him) said: "There is no sin more recurring punishment (very rapidly) in the present life, along with what awaits for its doer in the Hereafter, than transgression and severing the ties of relationship."

Eve gave birth to 40 children through twenty births. Others said: there were 120 births, in each one a male and a female were born. The first among them were Cain and his sister Qalimah, and the last ones were Abdul Mughith and his sister Ummul Mughith. Then, humans increased in number and spread into the earth. Allah Almighty said: "O mankind! Be dutiful to your Lord, Who created you from a single person (Adam), and from him (Adam) He created his wife [Hawwa (Eve)], and from them both He created many men and women; fear Allah through Whom you demand (your mutual rights), and (do not cut the relations of) the wombs (kinship). Surely, Allah is Ever an All-Watcher over you." (An-Nisa, 1)

Historians said: Adam did not die till he saw from among his progeny and offspring 400,000. Only Allah knows best!

Adam (Peace be upon him) had no father or mother. Allah made the Angels prostrate themselves before him, Who taught Adam names of everything, and Who made him dwell in His spacious Paradise. The Messenger of Allah said: "There were 124,000 Prophets and 315 Messengers. Adam was the first Messenger (peace be upon him). Adam was also sent with a Message. Allah the Almighty created him with His Hand, then, breathed into him out of His Soul, then, He fashioned him (in a very proper manner)."

Every messenger is a prophet, but every prophet is not a messenger. A prophet is a person who receives Divine message via revelation but is not supposed to preach it and in other words to convey this message to the people. But a messenger is a person who in addition to receiving revelation he should disseminate that message and convey it to the people. The former is referred to as Nabi in Islam while the latter is referred to as Rasool.

In the Night Journey, the Prophet (Peace be upon him) said: "The gate was opened, then we went to the nearest heaven and there we saw a man sitting with some people on his right and some on his left. When he looked towards his right, he laughed and when he looked towards his left he wept. The man then said: 'Welcome! O'Pious Prophet and pious son!' I asked Gabriel: 'Who is he?' He replied: 'He is Adam and the people on his right and left are the souls of his offspring. Those on his right are the people of Paradise and those on his left are the people of Hell and when he looks towards his right he laughs and when he looks towards his left he weeps.'"

The Prophet (peace be upon him) said: "Then, I passed by Yusuf (Joseph) and I found him to be granted half of beauty." Some scholars explained that it means that he was given half of the beauty Adam was granted. Indeed, this is very suitable and convincing! That Allah, the Almighty created Adam, fashioned him by His Hand and breathed into him out of His Soul, for all these Allah the Almighty must have created the best of all things. When Allah created Paradise, the Angels said: "Our Lord! Make this for us for You created for mankind the present world in which they eat and drink."
Allah said: "By My Glory and Loftiness! I will not equalize between the pious from among those whom I created with My Hand, and those whom When I said "Be! They

were!"

The Messenger of Allah (Peace be upon him) said: "Allah, the Exalted and Glorious created Adam in His own image with His length of 60 cubits. He told Adam to greet the angels, and listen to the response that they give him, for it would form his greeting and that of his offspring. Adam then addressed them: Peace be upon you! They (the angels) said: May there be peace upon you and the Mercy of Allah, and they made an addition of 'Mercy of Allah.' So he who would get into Paradise would get in the form of Adam, his length being 60 cubits, then the people who followed him continued to diminish in size up to this day."

The Story of Marut and Harut (2)

Allah the Almighty said:

"They followed what the Shayatin (the devils) taught them (falsely of the magic) in the lifetime of Prophet Suleiman (Solomon) (peace be upon him). Suleiman did not disbelieve or disobey Allah, but the Shayatin (devils) disbelieved, teaching men magic and such things that came down at Babylon to the two angels, Marut and Harut. Neither Marut nor Harut taught anyone such things. People learned that by which they cause separation between man and his wife, but they could not harm anyone except by Allah's Leave. And they learned that which harms them and profits them not. And indeed they knew that the buyers of the magic would have no share in the Hereafter. If they had believed and guarded themselves from evil and kept their duty to Allah, far better would have been for them."
(Al-Baqarah, 102, 103)

When Suleiman lost his kingdom, great numbers from among mankind and the jinn renegaded and followed their lusts. But, when Allah restored to Suleiman his kingdom, the renegade came to follow the Straight Path once again. Prophet Suleiman seized their holy scriptures which he buried underneath his throne. Shortly after, Prophet Suleiman (peace be upon him) died. In no time, the men and the Jinn uncovered the buried scriptures and said: This was a book revealed by Allah to Suleiman who hid it from us. Then they took it as their religion and Allah said: "And when there came to them a Messenger from Allah confirming what was with them, a party of those who were given the Scripture threw away the Book of Allah behind their backs as if they did not know." (Al-Baqarah, 101) and they followed what the devils gave out, i.e., musical instruments, etc.

Asif was Suleiman's scribe. He knew the Greatest Name of Allah and used to write what he was ordered to by Suleiman, then, bury it underneath the throne. After Suleiman's death, the devils got it out and wrote between each two lines magical and blasphemous things.

They said: "This is what Suleiman used to apply and act upon." The ignorant among the people regarded Suleiman as a disbeliever and continued to insult him until Prophet Muhammad (Peace be upon him) was sent with the Glorious Quran that reads.

When Suleiman wanted to answer the call of nature or wanted to be with any of his wives, he used to give his ring to a woman called Al-Jaradah. Afterwards, Satan came to her in the form of Suleiman and took the ring from her. When Satan put the ring on, all mankind, the jinn and Devils submitted to him. Then, when Suleiman came seeking his ring from her, she said: "You are not Suleiman." Thus, Suleiman knew that it was a test from Allah the Almighty. Upon this, the devils were free to do whatever they wished. So, they wrote down books of black magic and blasphemy which they buried underneath the throne of Suleiman. When Suleiman's died, they uncovered these books and said to the people: This is what Suleiman used to do with the help of these books. Consequently, the people declared their innocence of Suleiman and declared him to be a disbeliever until the advent of Prophet Muhammad (peace and blessings be upon him) who came with the Quranic Verse that says: "Suleiman did not disbelieve, but the Shayatin (devils) disbelieved."

Allah the Almighty informed Prophet Suleiman (peace be upon him) with the matter and enabled him to bury these lies under his throne. After his death, one of the devils said: "I can lead you to Suleiman's dearest and most precious treasure. It is under his throne." Consequently, they uncovered it and said: "This is magic." Afterwards, it continued to be copied and acted upon. The people believed in them and regarded them trustworthy. Time after time, the soothsayers trusted the devils who later on used to add to each word one-hundred lies of their own. The people started to write down these matters and it circulated among the Children of Israel that the Jinn knew the Unseen. Suleiman moved quickly and gathered all these writings and put them in a chest and buried it under his throne. All the devils who tried to even approach the chest were burnt alive. Suleiman declared that he would behead anyone who claims that the devils knew the Unseen.

Suleiman used to look for and capture the magic of the devils and keep it buried under his throne. The devils could not reach it and thus they inspired to the people that it is the knowledge with which Suleiman was able to overcome the Jinn, the wind, etc., and that it is buried under his own throne. Afterwards, the people got it out and practiced it. Later, the people of the Hejaz said: Suleiman used to practice sorcery.

When Prophet Muhammad (Peace and blessing be upon him) was sent and he mentioned Dawud and Suleiman, the Jews said: "Muhammad confounds the truth with falsehood: he puts Suleiman with the Prophets while he was just a sorcerer who was carried by the wind."

Allah the Almighty said: "They followed what the Shayatin (devils) gave out (falsely of the magic) in the lifetime of Suleiman (Solomon). Suleiman did not disbelieve, but the Shayatin (devils) disbelieved, teaching men magic and such things that came down at Babylon to the two angels, Harut and Marut."

Prophet Suleiman (Peace be upon him) took from every living creature a covenant. So when any person got afflicted with anything, Prophet Suleiman asked Allah with that covenant and the person recovered. Unfortunately, the people added to this sorcery and magic and said: this is what Suleiman Ibn Dawud used to act upon.

It is true that magic existed before the time of Prophet Suleiman (Peace be upon them) because magicians lived in the lifetime of Musa (Moses) (Peace be upon him) and Prophet Suleiman came after Musa (Peace be upon them both). Allah the Almighty said: "Have you not thought about the group of the Children of Israel after (the time of) Musa (Moses)? When they said to a Prophet of theirs, 'Appoint for us a king and we will fight in Allah's Way.' He said, 'Would you then refrain from fighting, if fighting was prescribed for you?' They said, 'Why should we not fight in Allah's Way while we have been driven out of our homes and our children (families have been taken as captives)?'

When Prophet Adam (Peace be upon him) was put down on earth, the angels said: "Lord! Will You place therein those who will make mischief therein and shed blood, while we glorify You with praises and thanks and sanctify You". (Al-Baqarah, 30) They continued: "Our Lord! We obey You more than man does."

Allah the Almighty said to them: "Appoint two angels from amongst you to descend to earth. The angels said: Our Lord! (We chose) Marut and Marut. They went down to earth where the flower appeared to them in the form of the most beautiful woman on earth. They asked her to be with them. But, she said: "Only after you disbelieve in Allah." They refused and she went away for a while. Then, she came back holding a child in her arms and they asked her for the second time. She said: "first, you must kill this boy." They refused to and she went away for a while and then, came back holding a glass of wine. They asked her for the third time. She said: "First, you must drink this glass of wine." They drank the wine, committed bad things with her and they also killed the boy. When they restored their conscience, the woman said: "By Allah! After you had drunk the wine, you committed all that which you refused to do at first." Thereupon, they were given the choice between receiving the torment of this life or that of the Hereafter. So they chose that of the present life."

Whosoever goes to a soothsayer or a magician and believes in what they say, they would become a disbeliever in what has been sent to Prophet Muhammad (Peace be upon him).

The Prophet (Peace and blessings be upon him) said: "Iblis places his throne upon water. He then sends detachments (for creating dissension). The nearer to him in rank are those who are most notorious in creating dissension. One of them comes and says: "I did so and so." And he says: "You have done nothing." Then one amongst them comes and says: "I did not spare so and so until I sowed the seed of discord between a husband and a wife."

Satan goes near him and says: "You have done well." He then embraces him. The dissension between a husband and his wife can be created through magic in that the devil let each one of them imagine something bad about the other. However, the devils cannot harm anyone except by Allah's Leave and Decree.

It was narrated that Al-Walid Ibn Uqbah had a magician who used to entertain him. He used to cut off a man's head, then calls it to get back to its proper place. The people said: "Glory be to Allah!" The magician revives the dead. However, a man from the pious migrants saw him and intended something. The next day he came and cut the magician's head and said: "if he is truthful, he can revive himself!" And, he recited Allah's Statement that reads: "Will you submit to magic while you see it." (Al-Anbiya, 4) Consequently, Al-Walid raged because the man did not ask for his permission first (to kill the magician), so he imprisoned him, but then later set him free. Allah knows best!

The Story of Dwellers of the Town (3)

Allah the Almighty said:

"And put forward to them a similitude: the (story of the) dwellers of the town, when there came Messengers to them. When We sent to them two Messengers, they belied them both; so We reinforced them with a third, and they said: "Verily we have been sent to you as Messengers." They (the people of the town) said: "You are only human beings like ourselves and the Most Gracious (Allah) has revealed nothing. You are only telling lies." The Messengers said: "Our Lord knows that we have been sent as Messengers to you." And our duty is only to convey plainly (the Lord's Message)." They (the people) said: "For us, we see an evil omen from you: if you cease not, we will surely stone you to death, and a painful torment will touch you from us." They (the Messengers) said: "Your evil omens be with you! (Do you call it 'evil omen') because you are admonished? Nay, but you are a people Musrifun (transgressing all bounds by committing all kinds of great sins, and by disobeying Allah)."

And there came a man running from the farthest part of the town. He said: "O'My people! Obey the Messengers. Obey those who ask no wages of you (for themselves), and who are rightly guided. And why should I not worship Him (Allah Alone) Who has created me and to Whom you shall be returned. Shall I take besides Him alihah (gods)? If the Most Gracious (Allah) intends me any harm, their intercession will be of no use for me whatsoever, nor can they save me? Then verily, I should be in plain error. Verily! I have believed in your Lord, so listen to me!" It was said (to him when the disbelievers killed him): "Enter Paradise." He said: "Would that my people knew. That my Lord (Allah) has forgiven me, and made me of the honored ones!"

And We sent not against his people after him a host from the heaven, nor was it needful for Us to send (such a thing). It was but one Saihah (shout) and lo! They (all) were still (silent, dead, destroyed). (Ya-Sin, 13-29)

Abdullah Ibn Abbas, Ka'b Al-Ahbar and Wahb Ibn Munabih and many others narrated a story of a town called Antioch (Antakiyah), governed by the king Antikhis Ibn Antikhis. This king used to observe idol worship. Allah Almighty sent him three Messengers whom he severely belied. The Messengers were: Sadiq, Masduq and Shalom.

It is evidently apparent that they were Messengers sent by Allah. Qatadah claimed them to be messengers sent by Jesus Christ. The same view was held by Ibn Jarir after Wahb after Ibn Suleiman after Shuaib Al-Jibai who added that: those messengers were called: Shimon, Jonah and Paul and the town was called Antioch.

This view is groundless because the people of Antioch when received three of the disciples of Jesus Christ (peace be upon him) were the first to believe in him at that very time. Thereupon, Antioch was one of the first 4 towns in which there first existed Christian Patriarchs. These 4 towns were Antioch, Jerusalem, Alexandria and Rome. However, the people of these towns were not destroyed, whereas the people of the aforementioned town in the Quranic verses were totally annihilated, following the killing of their companion whom Allah sent to admonish them.

Allah the Almighty said: "It was but one Saihah (shout)! They (all) were still (silent, dead and destroyed)." (Ya-Sin, 29)

There is no contradiction between the two interpretations, if the case was that the three Messengers of Allah were sent to the earlier dwellers of Antioch and that they were belied, the matter which incurred complete destruction. Then, their land was re-inhabited and during the lifetime of Jesus (Peace be upon him) the new dwellers believed in his three messengers.

Allah the Almighty says: "And there came a man running from the farthest part of the town, to support the Messengers and to declare his faith in them. He said: "O'My people! Obey the Messengers. Obey those who ask no wages of you (for themselves), and who are rightly guide."

Then he invited them to worship Allah Alone, and not to worship other than Him that can do nothing in this present life or in the Hereafter.

Then, the believing man said to the 3 Messengers: "Verily! I have believed in your Lord, so listen to me!" Thereupon, the people killed him by stoning him and stepping over his body until they broke his neck. The name of that believing man was Habib Ibn Murriy who was said to be a carpenter, or rope-maker, or shoe-maker. It is also said that he used to observe his religious rituals in an isolated cave. Abdullah Ibn `Abbas (May Allah be pleased with him) said: He was Habib, the carpenter who was afflicted with leprosy. He was charitable, but killed at the end at the hands of his own people. Then, Allah the Almighty says: "Enter Paradise." When he saw of the pleasures and joys therein, he said: "Would that my people knew? That my Lord (Allah) has forgiven me, and made me of the honored ones!"
Allah the Almighty sent Gabriel (Peace be upon him) who maintained a grasp on their town's gate and made a single shout [one Saihah (shout)]! They (all) were still (silent, dead, destroyed)), i.e. they turned to be silent, motionless and dead.

Finally, all these indicate that the town mentioned in the Quranic verses was not

Antioch because the people of Antioch believed in Allah and followed the messengers of Jesus (Peace be upon him). Moreover, Antioch was said to be the first town to declare faith in Jesus (Peace be upon him).

The Story of the Heifer (4)

Allah the Almighty said:

And (remember) when Musa (Moses) said to his people: "Allah commands you that you slaughter a cow." They said: "Do you make fun of us?" Moses said, "I take Allah's refuge from being among Al-Jahilun (the ignorant, the foolish)." They said: "Call upon your Lord for us that He may make plain to us what it is!" Moses said, "He says: It is a cow neither too old nor too young, but (it is) between the two conditions, so do what you are commanded." They said: "Call upon your Lord for us to make plain to us its color." Moses said: "He says it is a yellow cow, bright in its color, pleasing the beholders." They said, "Call upon your Lord for us to make plain to us what it is. Verily, to us all cows are alike. And surely, if Allah wills, we will be guided." Moses said: "He says: It is a cow neither trained to tilt the soil nor water the fields. It having no other color except bright yellow." They said: "Now you have brought the truth." So they slaughtered it though they were near to not doing it. And (remember) when you killed a man and fell into dispute among yourselves as to the crime. But Allah brought forth that which you were hiding. So We said: "Strike him (the dead man) with a piece of it (the cow). Thus Allah brings the dead to life and shows you His Aya: (proofs, evidences, verses, lessons, signs, revelations, etc.) so that you may understand." (Al-Baqarah, 67- 73)

Abdullah Ibn Abbas and other scholars said: An old man from among the Children of Israel was very rich, and he had some nephews who wished he would die soon to inherit him. One day, one of them killed him at night and threw him on the road, or at the door of one of his own brothers. In the morning, the people found the dead body and they disputed over him. His nephew, the murderer, came and began to weep and to cry. Some people said: "Why do you dispute over him? Why do not you go to Allah's Prophet (Peace be upon him)?"

So his nephew went and complained to Moses (peace be upon him). Moses said: "By Allah! Anyone who knows anything about this murdered man, he should let us know." But, no one knew anything about it. Thereupon, they asked Moses (peace be upon him) to ask his Lord concerning this issue. Moses (peace be upon him) asked his Lord and he was commanded to order them to slaughter a cow, "Verily, Allah commands you that you slaughter a cow. They said: "Do you make fun of us?"

Moses said: "I take Allah's Refuge from being among Al-Jahilun (the ignorant, the foolish). I take Allah's Refuge from saying other than that He revealed to me, and that was His Answer to what you had wanted me to ask Him."

Ibn Abbas and others said: If they were to slaughter any cow, they would fulfill the purpose thereof. But, they made it difficult for themselves (by asking so many questions thereof), and thus Allah the Almighty made it difficult for them (by stipulating so many conditions for the desired cow). They asked about its description, color and age, and they were answered with what was scarce and dear (in a way to make it hard for them to find it). The point is that they were commanded to slaughter neither a too old cow, nor a too young, but (it is) between the two conditions. But they pressed themselves with their questions through asking about its color. And they were answered to make it yellow cow, bright in its color, pleasing the beholders, which is very rare and dear.

They said: "Call upon your Lord for us to make plain to us what it is. Verily, to us all cows are alike. And surely, if Allah wills, we will be guided." Moses said: "He says: It is a cow neither trained to tilt the soil nor water the fields, sound, having no other color except bright yellow." They said: "Now you have brought the truth." So they slaughtered it though they were near to not doing it. It is said that they could not find a cow with all these descriptions but with a man who was righteous and good to his father. They asked him to submit it to them, but he refused. They tried to seduce him as to its price till they offered him what equals its weight in gold. But, he refused. Then, they offered him an amount of gold that equals its weight 10 times. Finally, he accepted their offer and submitted it to them. Then, Moses (Peace be upon him) commanded them to slaughter it. So they slaughtered it though they were near to not doing it, i.e. while they were still hesitant.

Then, Moses (Peace be upon him) instructed them with the Command of Allah to strike the dead man with a piece of the cow. Some scholars said they struck the man with part of its thighbone, or with part of the flesh between its shoulders. When they struck him with part thereof, he was resurrected by Allah the Almighty. Moses (Peace be upon him) asked him: "Who killed you? He said: "It was my nephew who killed me." Then, he died again. Allah the Almighty says: "Thus Allah brings the dead to life and shows you His Ayat (proofs, evidences, verses, lessons, signs, revelations, etc.) so that you may understand," i.e. as you witnessed the revival of that dead man by the Command of Allah the Almighty. He can do the same to all the dead people when He wishes to. Allah said: "The creation of you all and the resurrection of you all are only as (the creation and resurrection of) a single person. (Luqman, 28)

The Story of Moses and Al-Khadir (5)

Allah the Almighty said:

And remember when Moses said to his servant: "I shall not give up travelling till I reach the junction of the two seas, or till I spent years and years in travelling." But when he reached the junction of the two seas, he forgot his fish. So when they had passed further away, Moses said to his servant: "Bring us our morning meal for truly we have suffered much fatigue in this journey." I forgot the fish, none but Satan made me forget it!" Moses said: "So he went back retracing his footsteps. Then he found one of Our slaves, on whom We had taught knowledge from Us. Moses said to him (Al-Khadir): "May I follow you so that you can teach me something of that knowledge which you have been taught by Allah?"

Al-Khadir said: "Verily you will not be able to have patience! And how can you have patience about things which you know not." Moses said: "You will find me patient, and I will not disobey you." Al-Khadir said: If you follow me, do not ask me about anything until I myself mention it."

So they both proceeded, then they boarded a ship, but then Al-Khadir scuttled it. Moses said: "Have you scuttled it to drown its people? Verily, you have committed an evil bad thing." Al-Khadir said: "Did I not tell you that you will not be able to have patience?" Moses said: "Call me not to account for what I forgot and do not be hard on me." Then they both proceeded until they met a boy, then Al-Khadir killed the boy. Moses said: "Have you killed an innocent boy. Verily, you have committed an evil dreadful thing)!" Al- Khadir said: "Did I not tell you that you can have no patience."

The Prophet (peace be upon him) said: "Allah would forgive His servant's evil bad deeds as long as they do not act on them, or speak about them." The Prophet (peace be upon him) said: "If anyone eats something forgetfully while they are fasting, then they should complete their fast, for Allah made them eat or drink."

Moses said: "If I ask you about anything after this, keep me not in your company." Then they both proceeded, until they came to the people of a town, they asked them for food, but they refused. Then they found a wall about to collapse so Al-Khadir set it up straight. Moses said: "You could have taken wages for it!"

Al-Khadir said: "This is the parting between us. I will explain now about those things over which you were unable to hold patience. As for the ship, it belonged to poor people that were working in the sea. I damaged it because there was a king behind them who seized every ship by force. I do not want them killed. And as for the boy, his parents loved Allah and Allah loved them. We feared he would oppress them by rebellion and disbelief. Allah wanted to change him for one better in righteousness and nearer to mercy. And as for the wall, it belonged to two orphan boys. Under the wall there is a treasure belonging to them. Their father was a very righteous person. Your Lord intended that they should attain their age of full strength and take out their treasure as a mercy from your Lord. I did not do anything of my own accord. This is the interpretation of those things for which you could not hold patience." (Al-Kahf, 60-82)

The Messenger of Allah (peace be upon him) said: "Once Moses stood up and addressed Banu Israel. He was asked: "Who is the most learned man amongst the people?" Moses said: "I am the most learned." So Allah admonished Moses, as he did not attribute absolute knowledge to Him (Allah). So Allah inspired to him, "That there is a slave of mine who is more learned than you." Moses said: "O my Lord! How can I meet him?" Allah Almighty said: "Take a fish in a large basket and proceed and you will find him at the place where you will lose the fish." So Moses set out along with his servant boy, Yusha bin Nun and carried a fish in a large basket until they reached a rock where they slept. The fish came out of the basket and it took its way into the sea.

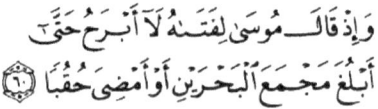

Then Moses and his servant boy proceeded for the rest of that night and the following day. When the day broke, Moses said to his servant boy: bring us our early meal. No doubt, we have suffered much fatigue in this journey. Moses did not get tired until he passed the place about which he was told. There the servant boy told Moses: "Do you remember when we betook ourselves to the rock, I indeed forgot the fish." Moses replied: "That is what we have been seeking." So they went back retracing their footsteps, until they reached the rock. There they saw a man covered with a garment. Moses greeted him.

Al-Khadir replied saying: "How do people greet each other in your land?" Moses said: "I am Moses." He asked: "The Moses of Banu Israel?" Moses replied in the affirmative and added: "May I follow you so that you teach me of that knowledge which you have been taught." Al-Khadir replied: "Verily! You will not be able to remain patient with me! I have some of the knowledge of Allah which He has taught me and which you do not know, while you have some knowledge which Allah has taught you which I do not know."

Moses said: "Allah willing, you will find me very patient and I will not disobey you." So both of them set out walking along the seashore, as they did not have a boat. In the meantime, a boat passed by them, and so they asked the boat's crew if they go with them. The crew recognized Al-Khadir and took them on board without fare. Then a sparrow came and stood on the edge of the boat and dipped its beak once or twice in the sea. Al-Khadir said: "O Moses! My knowledge and your knowledge have not decreased Allah's knowledge except as much as this sparrow has decreased the water of the sea with its beak." Al-Khadir then went to one of the planks of the boat and plucked it out. Moses said: "These people gave us a free lift but you have broken their boat and scuttled it so as to drown its people." Al-Khadir replied: "I told you that you will not be able to remain patient with me." Moses said: "Call me not to account for what I forgot." The first (excuse) of Moses was that he had forgotten. Then they proceeded further and found a boy playing with other boys. Al-Khadir took hold of the boy's head from the top and plucked it out with his hands (killed him). Moses said: "You have killed an innocent soul who has killed none."

Al-Khadir replied: "I told you that you would not remain patient with me?" Then they both proceeded until when they came to the people of a town, they asked them for food, but they refused to entertain them. Then they found there a wall on the point of falling down. Al-Khadir repaired it with his own hands. Moses said: "If you had wished, you could have taken wages for it." Al-Khadir replied: "This is the parting between you and me."

$$\text{فَانْطَلَقَا حَتَّىٰ إِذَا أَتَيَا أَهْلَ قَرْيَةٍ اسْتَطْعَمَا أَهْلَهَا فَأَبَوْا أَن يُضَيِّفُوهُمَا فَوَجَدَا فِيهَا جِدَارًا يُرِيدُ أَن يَنقَضَّ فَأَقَامَهُ ۖ قَالَ لَوْ شِئْتَ لَتَّخَذْتَ عَلَيْهِ أَجْرًا ۝}$$

Allah the Almighty says: "And as for the wall, it belonged to two orphan boys in the town." As Suhaili said: they were Asram and Sarim sons of Kashih. And there was under it a treasure belonging to them. The treasure was gold, or some kind of knowledge." However, the most likely view is that it was some kind of knowledge inscribed on a golden board.

Al-Bazzar said: I was told that the treasure mentioned in Allah's Book (the Glorious Quran) was a solid golden board where it was inscribed: "I wondered at the one who affirmed faith in the Divine Decree and then he exerted himself; and I wondered at the one who remembered Hell-Fire and then he laughed, and I wondered at the one who remembered death and then he became heedless of the meaning of 'There is no god but Allah.'"

This proves that the righteousness of the father benefits his own children and their children.

Al-Khadir's Name, Lineage and Prophethood: Is He Still Alive? The real name, lineage and status of Al-Khadir are controversial. This can be added to the very important question: is he still alive?

Al-Hafiz Ibn Asakir said: He is said to be Al-Khadir son of Adam. Ibn Qutaibah said: His name was Balya or Aylya Ibn Malakan Ibn Faligh Ibn bir Ibn Shalikh Ibn Arfakhshdh Ibn Sam Ibn Noah (Peace be upon him).

Others said: He is Khadrun Ibn Amyaiyl Ibn Al-afiz Ibn Al-Iys Ibn Ishaq Ibn Prophet

Ibrahim peace be upon him). There are so many other views pertaining to his name and lineage.

Imam Al-Bukhari said: I was told by Muhammad Ibn Sa'id Al-Asbahani after Ibn Al-Mubarak after Muamir after Hammam on the authority of Abu Hurairah (May Allah be pleased with him) that the Prophet (Peace and blessings be upon him) said: "Al- Khadir was named so because he sat over a barren white land, it turned green with plantation after (his sitting over It)."

Qabisah narrated on the authority of Ath-Thauri after Mansur after Mujahid as saying: Al-Khadir was named so because everything around him used to turn into green when he stands for prayer. It was stated earlier that Moses and

Yusha (Peace be upon them) went back retracing their footsteps, until they reached the rock. There they saw a man covered with a green garment. Moses greeted him. Al-Khadir replied saying: "How do people greet each other in your land?" Moses said: "I am Moses." He asked: "The Moses of Banu Israel?" Moses replied in the affirmative and added: "May I follow you so that you teach me of that knowledge which you have been taught... etc."

The Story Indicated His Prophethood in Four Aspects:

First: Allah the Almighty says: "Then they found one of Our slaves, on whom We had bestowed mercy from Us, and whom We had taught knowledge from Us." (Al-Kahf, 65)

Second: Moses says to Al-Khadir: "May I follow you so that you teach me something of that knowledge (guidance and true path) which you have been taught (by Allah)?" He (Al-Khadir) said: "Verily you will not be able to have patience with me! And how can you have patience about a thing which you know not."
Moses said: "If Allah wills, you will find me patient, and I will not disobey you in aught." He (Al-Khadir) said: "Then, if you follow me, ask me not about anything till I myself mention of it to you".

So, were he not a Prophet, Moses would not address him that way, and he would not answer Moses that way as well. Moses sought his company because he wanted to get some of the knowledge Al-Khadir was given by Allah and that which Moses did not get. Were Al-Khadir anything but a Prophet, he would not be infallible.

Thus, Moses would not be keen to accompany him because Moses himself was an honorable Prophet and an infallible Messenger. Were Al-Khadir anything but a Prophet, Moses would not take the trouble of searching for him for 8 years. When Moses met with Al-Khadir, Moses highly respected him and followed him submissively to gain as much as possible of his divine knowledge.

Third: Al-Khadir intentionally killed the boy. He would not do that without an inspiration from Allah Almighty ordering him to. This incident can stand as a separate proof that Al-Khadir was a Prophet. It can stand as well, as a proof that he was infallible. Al-Khadir killed the boy because he was inspired that the boy would be a disbeliever when he grows up and that his parents would follow him due to their earnest love for him. So he killed him to save the faith of the parents. This indicated that he was an infallible Prophet.

Fourth: When Al-Khadir interpreted and explained for Moses the actions he took and clarified everything to him he added: "As a mercy from your Lord. And I did them not of my own accord)," i.e. I did not do that out of my desire, instead, I was ordered to by divine inspiration. All these indicated his Prophethood and infallibility.

Is Al-Khadir Still Alive?

The majority of scholars said: "Al-Khadir is still alive because he was the one who buried Adam (Peace be upon him) after the Deluge and thus he was affected by the invocation of Adam that he who buries him will live long." Some people said: "he is still alive because he drank of the spring of life."

There are so many narrations and stories on which those who viewed the existence of Al-Khadir today based their opinion. But, all the narrations and Hadiths pertaining to that issue are weak and invented and those who narrated them are not infallible. Abdur Razzaq said: "I was told by Mu amir that Abu Sa'id Al-Khudri said: "One day Allah's Messenger (Peace be upon him) narrated to us a long narration about Ad-Dajjal and among the things he narrated to us, was: Ad-Dajjal will come, and he will be forbidden to enter the mountain passes of Medina.

He will encamp in one of the salt areas neighboring Medina and there will appear to him a man who will be the best or one of the best of the people. He will say: 'I testify that you are Ad-Dajjal whose story Allah's Messenger has told us.' Ad Dajjal will say (to his audience): 'Look, if I kill this man and then give him life, will you have any doubt about my claim?'
They will reply: 'No.' Then Ad Dajjal will kill that man and then will make him alive. The man will say: 'By Allah, now I recognize you more than ever! 'Ad-Dajjal

will then try to kill him (again) but he will not be given the power to do so." Mu'amir said: "I was told that the man who stands against the Dajjal is Al-Khadir and that his neck on that day would be covered with brass."

Sheik Abu Al-Faraj Ibn Al-Jawzi refuted all these Hadiths and proved them all to be invented, and he proved the Chains of Transmission of the narrations and stories of the Prophet's Companions and followers to be weak and fallible. Indeed, Ibn Al-Jawzi was very powerful and authentic in doing so.

As for those who claimed Al-Khadir to be dead such as Imam Al-Bukhari, Abu Al-Husain Ibn Al-Munadi and sheik Abu Al-Faraj Ibn Al-Jawzi, they held as their textual proofs what follows:

Allah the Almighty says: "And We granted not to any human being immortality before you O'Muhammad (peace be upon him): then if you die, would they live forever?" (Al-Anbyia, 34)

So if Al-Khadir was a human being, he would be affected by this ruling: he is mortal, he must die. Allah the Almighty says: "And remember when Allah took the Covenant of the Prophets, saying: "Take whatever I gave you from the Book and Hikmah (understanding of the Laws of Allah), and afterwards there will come to you a Messenger (Muhammad (peace be upon him) confirming what is with you. You must, then, believe in him and help him." Allah said: "Do you agree to it and will you take up My Covenant (which I conclude with you)?"

They said: "We agree." He said: "Then bear witness; and I am with you among the witnesses (for this)." (Al Imran, 81)

Ibn Abbas (May Allah be pleased with him) said: "Allah took the Covenant of all the Prophets to believe in Muhammad and support him if he appears during their lifetimes. In addition, they should take the Covenant of all their own nations to believe in him and support him in the same way. Thereupon, were Al-Khadir a Prophet or a Wali (protector or guardian), he would be involved in that Covenant and that were he alive during the lifetime of Prophet Muhammad (Peace be upon him), he would follow him and present himself before him paying allegiance and absolute faith."

Imam Ahmed narrated: I was told by Shuraih Ibn An-Nu'man after Hashim after Mujalid after AshShi'bi after Jabir Ibn 'Abdullah that the Prophet (Peace be upon him) said: "By Him in Whose Hand my soul is! Were Moses alive, he would do nothing but follow me."

This is the decisive view which the earlier Quranic Verse indicates that all Prophets if they happen to live during the lifetime of Prophet Muhammad are ordered to follow him and practice his own Shariah. On the Night Journey, he (Peace be upon him) was raised far above them all. When they descended to Jerusalem and the time for Prayer was due, he (Peace be upon him) was ordered to lead them all (in Prayer). This showed that he is the greatest Imam and the last Prophet who is most honored and respected (May Allah grant him and them all mercy).

Thereupon, if Al-Khadir were alive, he would be joining forces with Prophet Muhammad (Peace be upon him), and he would follow his religion in every minute detail. This is Prophet Isa (Jesus) (Peace be upon him) when he will descends by the end of time, he will rule over the whole world in accordance with this honorable legislation of Prophet Muhammad (peace and blessings be upon him). However, there is nothing to certify that Al-Khadir has met together with Prophet Muhammad (Peace be upon him) in a single day or even witnessed any fight with him against the polytheists or the infidels.

On the day on which the Battle of Badr was fought, the Messenger of Allah (Peace be upon him) cast a glance at the infidels, and they were 1000, while his own Companions were 319. Allah's Prophet (peace and blessings be upon him) turned (his face) towards the Qiblah. Then, he stretched his hands and began his supplication to his Lord: 'O'Allah! Accomplish for me what Thou hast promised to me. O'Allah! Bring about what Thou hast promised to me. O'Allah! If this small band of Muslims is destroyed, Thou will not be worshipped on this earth.'

The Prophet (peace be upon him) continued his supplication to his Lord, stretching his hands, facing the Qiblah, until his mantle slipped down from his shoulders. So Abu Bakr (May Allah be pleased with him) came to him, picked up his mantle and put it on his shoulders. Then Abu Bakr embraced him from behind and said: "O'Prophet of Allah! This prayer of yours to your Lord will suffice you, and He will fulfil for you what He has promised you."

Allah said: "I will help you with a thousand of the angels each behind the other (following one another) in succession." (Al-Anfal, 9)
So Allah helped him with angels." (Sahih Muslim) However, this small band of Muslims consisted, then, of the chiefs from among the Muslims and the angels, foremost among whom was Jibril (Gabriel) (Peace be upon him). Thus, if Al-Khadir

were alive, his presence, then, would be the best thing he could ever do. Narrated Al-Qadi Abu Ya`la Muhammad Ibn Al-Husain Al- Fara Al-Hanbali: Some people asked some of our companions about Al-Khadir, was he dead? They answered: "Yes."

Some people claim that Al-Khadir was present during all these past events but no one could see him because he was invisible. Obviously, this claim is groundless and is based only on illusions. Indeed, if he was still alive during the lifetime of Prophet Muhammad (peace and blessings be upon him), he would certainly join them in fight against the polytheists of the tribe of Quraish. See the following Hadith: Narrated Sa'd (May Allah be pleased with him): "On the Day of Uhud I saw on the right side of Allah's Messenger (peace and blessings be upon him) and on his left side two persons dressed in white clothes and whom I did not see before nor after that, and they were Gabriel and Michael (may Allah be pleased with both of them)." (Sahih Muslim)

In addition, Abdullah Ibn Umar (May Allah be pleased with both of them) said: "Once the Prophet (Peace be upon him) led us in the Isha (Night) Prayer during the last days of his life and after finishing it (the Prayer) (with Taslim, i.e. final salutation) he said: 'Do you realize the importance of this night? None of you present on the surface of the earth tonight will be living after the completion of one hundred years from this night." Omar (RA) said: People were (not understanding) these words of the Messenger of Allah (peace and blessings be upon him) which had been uttered pertaining to one hundred years.

Allah's Messenger (Peace be upon him) in fact meant (by these words) that on that day none from amongst those who had been living upon the earth (from amongst his Companions) would survive (after one hundred years) and that would be the end of this generation." (Sahih Muslim)

And, Jabir Ibn `Abdullah (May Allah be pleased with him) reported: "I heard Allah's Messenger (Peace be upon him) as saying this one month before his death: 'You asked me about the Last Hour whereas its knowledge is with Allah. I, however, take an oath and say that none upon the earth, the created beings (from amongst my Companions), would survive at the end of one hundred years."

This Hadith has been narrated on the authority of Ibn Juraij with the same chain of transmitters, but there is no mention of the words: "one month before his death." (Sahih Muslim) So, even if Al-Khadir were alive during the lifetime of Prophet

Muhammad (Peace be upon him), he would, then, be dead in accordance with these above-mentioned Hadiths. And, Allah knows best!

The Story of Qarun (6)

Allah the Almighty said:

"Verily, Qarun was of Moses people, but Qarun behaved very arrogantly towards everyone. We had given him treasures that of which the keys would have been a burden to a body of strong men. Remember when his people said to him: 'Do not exult (with riches, being ungrateful to Allah). Verily Allah likes not those who exult (with riches, being ungrateful to Allah).' But seek with that wealth which Allah has bestowed on you, the home of the Hereafter, and forget not your portion of lawful enjoyment in this world, and do good as Allah has been good to you, and seek not mischief in the land. Verily, Allah likes not those who commit great crimes and sins, oppressors, tyrants, mischief-makers, corrupters."

He said: "It is not Allah. This has been given to me only because of the knowledge I possess." Did he not know that Allah had destroyed before him men who were stronger than him in might and greater in riches that they had once collected? The criminals, disbelievers, polytheists, sinners will not be questioned of their sins because Allah knows them well, so they will be punished without being called to account. So he went forth before his people in his pomp. Those who were desirous of the life of the world, said: 'Ah, would that we had the like of what Qarun has been given! Verily he is the owner of a great fortune.' But those who had been given religious knowledge said: 'Woe to you! The Reward of Allah in the Hereafter is far better for those who believe and do righteous good deeds, and this none shall attain except those who are the patient in following the truth.' So We caused the earth to swallow Qarun and his house and treasures. Then he had no group or party to help him against Allah, nor was he one of those who could save themselves.

Then those who had desired for a position like his position the day before, began to say: 'Know you not that it is Allah Who enlarges the provision or restricts it to whom-so-ever He pleases of His slaves. Had it not been that Allah was Gracious to us, He could have caused the earth to swallow us up also! Know you not that the disbelievers will never be successful.' That home of the Hereafter in Paradise. We shall assign to those who rebel not against the truth with pride and oppression in the land nor do mischief by committing crimes. And the good end is for the Muttaqun (righteous persons and the pious)." (Al-Qasas, 76-83)

Ibn Abbas (May Allah be pleased with him) held the opinion that Qarun was a paternal cousin to Moses (peace be upon him). This view is supported by many other narrators, including Ibn Juraij who added that he is Qarun Ibn Yashar Ibn Qahith, while Moses was the son of Imran Ibn Hafith. Ibn Juraij went further and rejected the viewpoint of Ibn Ishaq that he was a paternal uncle to Moses (peace be upon him).

Qatadah said: He was called "An-Nur" (the light) for he had a melodious voice while reciting the Torah (Taurat), but he became a hypocrite just like As-Samiri who became a hypocrite too. Thus, Qarun was destroyed because of his transgression due to the wealth and riches he had.

Shahr Ibn Haushab said: he dragged his garment out of pride and arrogance (conceit).

Allah the Almighty mentioned the numerousness of his wealth and riches so that its keys would have been a burden to a body of strong men. It was also said: the keys were made of leather and that they used to be carried on sixty mules. Allah knows best!

However, he was advised by the godly men from among his people saying: "Do not exult," i.e., do not be arrogant or conceited with riches, being ungrateful to Allah the Almighty. Verily Allah likes not those who are ungrateful.

Seek with that wealth which Allah has bestowed on you, the home of the Hereafter. They advise him to direct his endeavors to gain Allah's Reward in the Hereafter as it is the best of all rewards.

His answer to this good advice of his people was nothing but: "He said: This has been given to me only because of the knowledge I possess," i.e., I do not need what you have said or referred to, as Allah only gave me this for He knew that I deserve it and I am really qualified thereto. Moreover, were it not for that He loves me, He would not grant or give me this. However, Allah the Almighty refuted his statement saying: "Did he not know that Allah had destroyed before him generations, men who were stronger than him in might and greater in the amount of riches they had once collected? But the Mujrimun (criminals, disbelievers, polytheists, sinners) will not be questioned of their sins (because Allah knows them well, so they will be punished without being called to account)," i.e., We have destroyed before him generations because of their sins and bad deeds and that they were stronger than Qarun and they had more riches and children than him.

So, if what he said was true, We would not punish anyone of those who had more riches than him and his wealth and riches would not be a proof of Our love or care for him. Allah the Almighty says: "And it is not your wealth, nor your children that bring you nearer to Us (i.e., please Allah), but only he who believes (in the Islamic Monotheism), and does righteous deeds (will please Us).

There will be twofold reward for what they did, and they will reside in the high dwellings Paradise and in peace and security. (Saba, 37) and, He says: "Do they think that in wealth and children with which We enlarge them. We hasten unto them with good things. Nay, [it is a Fitnah (trial) in this worldly life so that they will have no share of good things in the Hereafter] but they perceive not). (Al-Mu'minun, 55, 56).

Allah's answer to Qarun's claims confirms our interpretation of his saying: "This has been given to me only because of the knowledge I possess."

But as for those who claimed that he was a chemist or that he knew the Greatest Name of Allah the Almighty and that he used it to collect wealth, all these are fallacies and not true. For chemistry cannot change the reality of something, and the Greatest Name is of no effect if it is pronounced by a disbeliever. And, Qarun was inherently a disbeliever and apparently a hypocrite. Moreover, the context of the advice given by his people and his answer to them do not support that claim.

Almighty Allah said: "So he went forth before his people in his pomp." Many interpreters mentioned that he went forth before his people in great luxuries: servants, clothes and riding animals. When those who were desirous of the life of the world saw him, they wished to have the same and wondered: "What a great fortune he has!" When their saying reached the ears of the godly righteous men they said to them: "Woe to you! The Reward of Allah is better for those who believe and do righteous good deeds," i.e., the Reward of Allah in the Hereafter is better and higher than this.

Almighty Allah said: "And this none shall attain except those who are As-Sabirun (patient in following the truth)," i.e., this -advice, saying and high determination regarding the Hereafter in presence of the joys of this present life. None shall attain except those who were guided and those whose hearts were fixed and minds made stable by the Grace of Allah the Almighty. And nothing is better than the saying of some of our earlier scholars who said: "Verily, Allah loves penetrative insight in time of suspicious matters and perfect reasoning in time of the presence of lusts."

Allah the Almighty said: "So, We caused the earth to swallow him and his dwelling place. Then, he had no group or party to help him against Allah, nor was he one of those who could save themselves". When Allah the Almighty mentioned his setting forth in his pomp. He said: "So We caused the earth to swallow him and his dwelling place."

As transmitted by Imam Al-Bukhari, Allah's Messenger (peace be upon him) said: "While a man was walking, clad in a two-piece garment and proud of himself with his hair well-combed, suddenly Allah made him sink into the earth and he will go on sinking into it till the Day of Resurrection." (Sahih Al-Bukhari)

Narrated Ibn Abbas (May Allah be pleased with him): Qarun gave a prostitute a sum of money to say to Moses (peace be upon him) while he is accompanied with other people that Moses committed with her adultery. It is said that she did it and consequently, Moses (peace be upon him) trembled with fear and he performed two Rakahs (bowing in prayer) and then said to her: "By Allah! Tell me, who hired you to do this? "She said: "It was Qarun who hired me to do that."

Then, she sought Allah's Forgiveness and repented to Him. Upon that, Moses (peace be upon him) prostrated himself and invoked Allah against Qarun. Allah the Almighty revealed to him that He subjugated the earth to obey him. Moses (peace be upon him) commanded the earth to swallow Qarun and his dwelling place. And it was! Allah knows best!
It was also said: That when Qarun went forth before his people in his pomp: guards,

mules and clothes, he passed by Moses (peace be upon him) while he was reminding the people of Allah. When the people saw him, the faces of most of them turned towards him. Moses (peace be upon him) called him and said: "Why do you do this?" Qarun replied saying: "You have been favored with Prophethood and I have been favored with riches. If you want, you may go forth and invoke Allah against me, and I would invoke Him against you." Thereupon, both of them went forth and Moses (peace be upon him) said: "Would you like to begin?" Qarun said: "Yes," and he made his invocations but they were not answered. When Moses (peace be upon him) invoked Allah the Almighty against him and said: "O Allah! Command the earth to transgress today." Allah revealed to him that He did. Then, Moses (peace be upon him) said: "O'Earth! Take them!" And it took them to their feet. Then, he said: "take them!" And it took them to their knees. Then, he said: "take them! And it took them to their shoulders." Then, he said: "O'Earth! Bring their riches and treasures! They were brought, then Moses pointed with his hand and said: "Go, you sons of Laui!" And they sank into the earth.

It was narrated from Qatadah that he said: "They would sink into the earth until the Day of Resurrection." Ibn Abbas (May Allah be pleased with him) said: "They sank into the earth till they reached the seventh earth."

Allah said: "Then he had no group or party to help him against Allah, nor was he one of those who could save themselves," i.e., he could not help himself or get help from others. "Then he will have no power, nor any helper." (At-Tariq, 10)
When the people saw what happened to Qarun and his treasures of sinking into the

earth and complete destruction, those who had desired for a position like his position the day before regretted and thanked Allah the Almighty and hence they said: "Had it not been that Allah was Gracious to us, He could have caused the earth to swallow us up also!

Then, Allah the Almighty told us that the home of the Hereafter, i.e., Paradise is prepared only for those who rebel not against the truth with pride and oppression in the land nor do mischief by committing crimes, and then He said: "And the good end is for the Muttaqun (the pious and righteous persons)."

This story of Qarun might have taken place before they get out of Egypt for Allah the Almighty said: "So, We caused the earth to swallow him and his dwelling place," or it might have taken place after. Allah knows best!

However, Almighty Allah mentions the dispraise of Qarun in several Verses on the Glorious Quran. Allah said: "And indeed We sent Moses with Our Ayat (proofs, evidences, verses, lessons, signs, revelations, etc.), and a manifest authority. To Firaun (Pharaoh), Haman and Qarun, but they called (him): 'A sorcerer, a liar!'" (Ghafir, 23, 24) and, in Surah Al-Ankabut after mentioning Ad, Thamud, Pharaoh, Haman and Qarun.

Allah said: "And We destroyed also Qarun, Firaun (Pharaoh), and Haman. And indeed Moses came to them with lessons, clear Ayat (proofs, evidences, verses, signs, revelations, etc.), but they were arrogant in the land, yet they could not outstrip Us. We punished each (of them) for his sins. We sent Hasib (a violent wind with shower of stones) [as on the people of Lut (Lot)], and of them were some who were overtaken by As-Saihah [torment, awful cry, (as Thamud or Shu'aib's People)], and of them were some whom We caused the earth to swallow [as Qarun], and of them were some whom We drowned [as the people of Nuh (Noah), or Firaun (Pharaoh) and his- people]. It was not Allah Who wronged them, but they wronged themselves." (Al-Ankabut, 39, 40) so, he who was swallowed by the earth was Qarun, and those whom were drowned were Pharaoh, Haman and their troops because they were sinful. Imam Ahmed, in his Musnad, reported that once the Messenger of Allah (peace and blessings be upon him) remembered the prayer and said: "He who observes it regularly and properly, it will be light, evidence and salvation for him on the Day of Resurrection. And, he who does not observe it regularly and properly, there will neither be for him -light, nor evidence, nor salvation. And, on the Day of Resurrection, he will be (gathered) with Qarun, Firaun (Pharaoh), Haman and Ubaiy Ibn Khalaf."

Bilqis (Queen of Sheba) (7)

Allah the Almighty said:

He inspected the birds, and said: 'What is the matter that I see not the hoopoe? Or is he among the absentees? I will surely punish him with a severe torment, or slaughter him, unless he brings me a clear reason.' But the hoopoe stayed not long: he (came up and) said: 'I have grasped (the knowledge of a thing) which you have not grasped and I have come to you from Saba (Sheba) with true news. I found a woman ruling over them: she has been given all things that could be possessed by any ruler of the earth, and she has a great throne. I found her and her people worshipping the sun instead of Allah, and Shaitan (Satan) has made their deeds fair-seeming to them, and has barred them from (Allah's) Way: so they have no guidance. [As Shaitan (Satan) has barred them from Allah's Way] so they do not worship (prostrate themselves before) Allah, Who brings to light what is hidden in the heavens and the earth, and knows what you conceal and what you reveal. Allah, La ilaha illa Huwa (none has the right to be worshipped but He), the Lord of the Supreme Throne!'

Suleiman (Solomon) said: 'We shall see whether you speak the truth or you are (one) of the liars. Go you with this letter of mine, and deliver it to them, then draw back from them, and see what (answer) they return.'

She said: 'O'Chiefs! Verily! Here is delivered to me a noble letter. Verily it is from Suleiman (Solomon), and verily, it (reads): In the Name of Allah, the Most Gracious, the Most Merciful: Be you not exalted against me, but come to me as Muslims (true believers who submit to Allah with full submission). She said: O'Chiefs! Advise me in (this) case of mine. I decide no case till you are present with me (and give me your opinions). They said: We have great strength, and great ability for war, but it is for you to command: so think over what you will command.

She said: 'Verily kings, when they enter a town (country), they despoil it and make the most honorable amongst its people the lowest. And thus they do. But verily! I am going to send him a present, and see with what (answer) the Messengers return.'

So when the messengers with the present came to Suleiman (Solomon), he said: 'Will you help me in wealth? What Allah has given me is better than that which He has given you! Nay, you rejoice in your gift!' [Then Suleiman (Solomon) said to the chief of her messengers who brought the present]: 'Go back to them. We verily shall come to them with hosts that they cannot resist, and we shall drive them out from there in disgrace, and they will be abased. He then said: "O chiefs! Which of you can bring me her throne before they come to me surrendering themselves in obedience?'

AIfrit (strong one) from the jinn said: 'I will bring it to you before you rise from your place (council). And verily, I am indeed strong, and trustworthy for such work.'

Buy one with whom was knowledge of the Scripture said: 'I will bring it to you within the twinkling of an eye!'

Then when Suleiman (Solomon) saw it placed before him, he said: 'This is by the Grace of my Lord to test me whether I am grateful or ungrateful! And whoever is grateful, truly, his gratitude is for (the good of) his own self, and whoever is ungrateful, (he is ungrateful only for the loss of his own self. Certainly my Lord is Rich (Free of all needs), Bountiful. He said: Disguise her throne for her that we may see whether she will be guided (to recognize her throne), or she will be one of those not guided.'

So when she came, it was said (to her): 'Is your throne like this?'
She said: 'It is, as though it were the very same.'

And [Suleiman (Solomon)] said: 'Knowledge was bestowed on us before her, and we were submitted to Allah (in Islam as Muslims before her). And that which she used to worship besides Allah has prevented her (from Islam), for she was of the disbelieving people.'

It was said to her: 'Enter As-Sarh,' (a glass surface with water underneath it or a palace), but when she saw it, she thought it was a pool, and she (tucked up her clothes) uncovering her legs.

Suleiman (Solomon) said: 'Verily, it is a Sarh (a glass surface with water underneath it or a palace).'

She said: 'My Lord! Verily, I have wronged myself, and I submit [in Islam, together with Suleiman (Solomon)] to Allah, the Lord of the
Alamin (mankind, jinn and all that exists).' (An-Naml. 20-44)

Allah the Almighty narrates what had happened between Suleiman and the hoopoe.

All kinds of birds had pioneers or chosen ones who were charged with certain tasks and who periodically attend themselves before Suleiman, as a habit of the troops with their kings. Ibn Abbas (May Allah be pleased with him) and others mentioned that the mission of the hoopoe was to search for water in deserts and barren areas. Indeed, the hoopoe has the ability as granted by Allah the Almighty to see and identify the locations of underground waters. Suleiman's hoopoe used to search for underground water and then to lead his troops thereto; they dig the land to get the water out and use it in fulfilling their needs.

One day, Suleiman (peace be upon him) wanted the hoopoe, he missed him and did not find him in his appointed position so, he said: "What is the matter that I see not the hoopoe? Or is he among the absentees? i.e., he is not here, or I cannot see him. I will surely punish him with a severe torment."

Suleiman (peace be upon him) threatened that he would punish him with some kind of penalty, or slaughter him, unless he brings me a clear reason, i.e., a clear excuse that may save him from my punishment.

Allah the Almighty said: "But the hoopoe stayed not long, i.e. his absence was not so long, then he (came up and) said to Suleiman (peace be upon him). I have grasped (the knowledge of a thing) which you have not grasped, i.e., I got to know that which you did not; and I have come to you from Saba (Sheba) with true news). That I found a woman ruling over them. She has been given all things that could be possessed by any ruler on earth, and she has a great throne. He is describing the status of the kings and rulers of Sheba in the Yemen. They had a mighty and glorious kingdom along with strong and competent troops. During that period, their king died and left no heirs but a daughter whom they raised as their queen."

Ath-Thalabi and others mentioned that after her father's death, the people appointed a man under whose rule corruption and mischief prevailed. She proposed to him in marriage and he married her. At their first night together she gave him wine till he got drunk and then she beheaded him and hanged his head on her door. Thereupon, the people raised her over the throne as their queen.

She was Bilqis Bint As-Sairah. Her father was called Al-Hudhad, or Shurahil Ibn Dhi Jadan Ibn As-Sairah Ibn Al-Harith Ibn Qais Ibn Saifi Ibn Saba Ibn Yashjub Ibn Ya rub Ibn Qahtan. Her father was one of the noblest kings. He refused to get married to Yemeni women. It is said that he got married to a woman from the Jinn whose name was Raihanah Bint As-Sakan who gave birth to that woman whose name is Balqamah, to be known later as Bilqis.

Ath-Thalabi transmitted on the authority of Sa`id Ibn Bashir on the authority of Qatadah after An-Nadr Ibn Anas after Bashir Ibn Nahik, after Abu Hurairah that Allah's Messenger (peace be upon him) said: "One of Bilqis's parents was from among the jinn." (This Hadith has some kind of Weakness).

Ath-Thalabi said: "I was told by Abu Abdullah Ibn Qabhunah on the authority of Abu Bakr Ibn Jarjah after Abu Bakrah as saying: 'Once, Bilqis was mentioned before Allah's Messenger (peace be upon him) who said: 'Such people as ruled by a lady will never be successful.'" (That sub-Narrator, Ismail Ibn Muslim is Meccan and he is regarded by the Scholars of Hadith as Weak, i.e. not an authentic narrator).

It is mentioned in Sahih Al-Bukhari from the narration of Auf on the authority of Al-Hasan, after Abu Bakra that: "When Allah's Messenger (peace be upon him) was informed that the Persians had crowned the daughter of Khusrau as their ruler, he said: 'Such people as ruled by a lady will never be successful.' (Sahih Al-Bukhari)

And, his saying that she has been given all things that could be possessed by any ruler of the earth, and she has a great throne, i.e., the chair she sits on was ornamented and studded with various jewels, pearls, gold and other magnificent things. Then, he mentioned their disbelief in Allah the Almighty and their worship of the sun instead of Allah and the deceivement of Satan to them by making their deeds look fair-seeming in their eyes, and barring them from Allah's Way.

So they do not worship (prostrate themselves before) Allah, Who brings to light what is hidden in the heavens and the earth, and knows what you conceal and what you reveal, i.e., He knows all secrets and revealed matters whether material or immaterial. Allah, La ilaha illa Huwa (none has the right to be worshipped but He), the Lord of the Supreme Throne! i.e., the Greatest Throne which none from among His creatures ever has.

Thereupon, Suleiman sent the hoopoe with a letter calling them to obey Allah and His Messenger, to repent and submit themselves to his kingship and power. He sent them and said: "Be you not exalted against me, i.e., do not let your pride prevent you from obeying me, but come to me as Muslims, i.e., true believers who submit to Allah with full submission."

The hoopoe dropped the letter near her and waited to see what she was going to do. However, she gathered the nobles, princes and ministers to have mutual consultation. She said: "O'Chiefs! Verily! Here is delivered to me a noble letter."

Then she first read its title, Verily it is from Suleiman (Solomon)), then she read the rest thereof and verily, it (reads): "In the Name of Allah, the Most Gracious, the Most Merciful: Be you not exalted against me, but come to me as Muslims (true believers who submit to Allah with full submission)."

Then she sought their advice in a very polite manner. She said: "O'Chiefs! Advise me in this case of mine. I decide no case till you are present with me, i.e., that you give me your opinions."

They said: "We have great strength, and great ability for war, i.e., we can afford war and all it needs of strength, materials, etc., so if you want this choice, we are well prepared thereto, but it is for you to command: so think over what you will command."

They showed full obedience to her and after showing and displaying their abilities before her they left the matter in her hands to see what should be done. Verily, her opinion was wiser and better than theirs as she knew that the sender of the letter was not to be resisted, fooled, or even deceived. She said: "Verily kings, when they enter a town (country), they despoil it and make the most honorable amongst its people the lowest. And thus they do, i.e. she explains to them that if that king overpowers this kingdom of theirs, she would be the one who receives the severest of punishment and degradation. But verily! I am going to send him a present, and see with what (answer) the Messengers return."
She wanted to bribe Suleiman with presents and gifts knowing that Suleiman (peace be upon him) would not accept from them but Islam, as she and her people were disbelievers while he and his troops are far stronger than them all. For this When (the messengers with the present) came to Suleiman (Solomon), he said: "Will you help me in wealth? What Allah has given me is better than that which He has given you! Nay, you rejoice in your gift!"

Then Suleiman (Solomon) said to the chief of her messengers who brought the present: "Go back to them. We verily shall come to them with hosts that they cannot resist, and we shall drive them out from there in disgrace, and they will be abased, i.e., go back with your gifts for what I have been granted by Allah is far better than these properties, riches and presents with which you rejoice and be filled with arrogance and pride over your own people. We verily shall come to them with hosts that they cannot resist, i.e., troops that are irresistible and cannot be defeated or encountered, and moreover we shall drive them out from their land, properties and wealth, in disgrace, and they will be abased, i.e., dragging shame, abasement and destruction."

When they heard the news, they rushed declaring their full submission and perfect obedience and willingness to accompany their queen in her leaving for meeting Suleiman (peace be upon him). When he (peace be upon him) heard of their coming and their intention to present themselves before his hand, he said to those (Jinn) from among his present hosts if they would bring him her throne before she manage to come. Alfrit (strong one) from the jinn said: "I will bring it to you before you rise from your place (council). And verily, I am indeed strong, and trustworthy for such work), i.e. before you finish your ruling council." It was said that he used to run the affairs of the Banu Israel from the beginning of the day till the noon. "Verily, I am indeed strong, and trustworthy for such work, i.e. I am strong enough to bring the throne to you, and at the same time I am to be entrusted with what it contains of the precious jewels and pearls."

But one with whom was knowledge of the Scripture then came. Asif Ibn Barkhiya who was Suleiman's maternal cousin, said it was one of the believers from among the Jinn who knew the Greatest Name of Allah the Almighty. It is also said that he was one from among the scholars of the Banu Israel. Moreover, it was said to be Suleiman himself, which is very strange and odd opinion and which As-Suhaili described to be out of context. A fourth opinion held that it was Gabriel (Peace be upon him. "I will bring it to you within the twinkling of an eye!" Before you send a messenger to the farthest place on earth and he comes back to you.

It was also said: "before the farthest person you can see reaches you, or before your sight gets weary of starring at some point and your eye closes; or before you regain your sight if you look to the farthest place your sight can reach then you close your eye, (which is the most likely interpretation)."

Then when Suleiman (Solomon) saw it placed before him, i.e., when he saw the throne of Bilqis brought and placed before him, in this too short period, from the Yemen to Jerusalem, he said: "This is by the Grace of my Lord to test me whether I am grateful or ungrateful! i.e. this is by the Grace of Allah lam granted and His Grace all people are granted testing them whether they are grateful or ungrateful. And whoever is grateful, truly, his gratitude is for (the good of) his own self, i.e., the benefit of this returns onto himself, and whoever is ungrateful, (he is ungrateful only for the loss of his own self. Certainly my Lord is Rich (Free of all needs), Bountiful, i.e., He is neither in need of thanking of the thankful, nor is He harmed by disbelief of the disbelievers."

Then, Suleiman (Peace be upon him) ordered her throne to be altered and disguised to test her mentality and understanding, saying that we may see whether she will be guided (to recognize her throne), or she will be one of those not guided. So when she came, it was said (to her): Is your throne like this?

She said: (It is) as though it were the very same, this is due to her understanding and clear insight that she set aside the possibility that it was her own throne for she has just left it far away in the Yemen, and that she did not know that there is any who can do this marvelous act of removing it to Jerusalem.

Allah the Almighty says pertaining to Suleiman (Peace be upon him) and his people And (Suleiman (Solomon)) said: Knowledge was bestowed on us before her, and we were submitted to Allah (in Islam as Muslims before her). And that which she used to worship besides Allah has prevented her (from Islam), for she was of a disbelieving people, i.e., worshipping the sun to whom she used to prostrate herself and her people instead of Allah the Almighty in follow of the religion of her fathers and ancestors with no evidence or proof of this.

Suleiman (peace be upon him) previously ordered a Sarh (a glass surface with water underneath in which there are various sorts of fish and other sea creatures) to be built. Afterwards, Bilqis was ordered to enter the Sarh while Suleiman (peace be upon him) was sitting on his throne.

But when she saw it, she thought it was a pool, and she tucked up her clothes uncovering her legs. Suleiman (Solomon) said: "Verily, it is a Sarh (a glass surface with water underneath it or a palace)."

She said: "My Lord! Verily, I have wronged myself, and I submit [in Islam, together with Suleiman (Solomon)] to Allah, the Lord of the Alamin (mankind, jinn and all that exists)."

It was said: That when Suleiman (peace be upon him) wanted to marry her he asked mankind about a way of removing the hair from her legs, and they mentioned the razor, but she feared thereof. Then, he (peace be upon him) consulted the Jinn who made the bath for him. Thus, he was the first to enter the bath.

At-Thalabi and others said: When Suleiman married her he returned the kingdom of Yemen to her and he used to visit her there and stay for three days a month then comes back to Jerusalem on the flying carpet. In addition, he ordered the Jinn to build him three palaces in the Yemen: Ghamdan, Salhin and Bitun. And, Allah knows best!

Ibn Ishaq transmitted after some scholars on the authority of Wahb Ibn Munabih that

Suleiman (Peace be upon him) did not marry her, but he got her married to the king of Ramadan and let her ruling over the Yemen again, and he (peace be upon him) subjected to her the king of the Jinn in Yemen to build her the aforementioned three palaces. This narration is not authenticated like the previous one, and Allah knows best!

The Story of Saba (Sheba) (8)

Allah the Almighty said:

Indeed there was for Saba (Sheba) a sign in their dwelling-place two gardens on the right hand and on the left. And it was said to them: "Eat of the provision of your Lord, and be grateful to Him. A fair land and an Oft-Forgiving Lord! But they turned away (from the obedience of Allah), so We sent against them Sail Al-Arim (flood re0leased from the dam), and We converted their two gardens into gardens producing bitter bad fruit, and tamarisks, and some few lote-trees. Like this We requited them because they were ungrateful disbelievers. And never do We requite in such a way except those who are ungrateful (disbelievers). And We placed, between them and the towns which We had blessed, towns easy to be seen, and We made the stages (of journey) between them easy (saying): 'Travel in them safely both by night and day.' But they said: 'Our Lord! Make the stages between our journey longer,' and they wronged themselves; so We made them as tales (in the land), and We dispersed them all totally. Verily, in this are indeed signs for every steadfast, grateful (person)." (Saba, 15-19)

Scholars of genealogy, among them was Muhammad Ibn Ishaq, said: "The name of Saba is Abd Shams Ibn Yashjub Ibn Yarub Ibn Qahtan. He was the first to take captives and he was very generous to the people."

As-Suhaili said: "It is said that he was the first person to be crowned, and some scholars said he was Muslim and that he composed poetry in which he brought good news to the advent of Prophet (peace and blessings be upon him). This last saying was attributed to Ibn Didya in his book titled: [At-Tanwir fi Maulid Al-Bashir An-Nadhir]

Imam Ahmed said: "I have been told by Abu Abdur Rahman, after Abdullah Ibn Luhaiah, after Abdullah Ibn Dalah saying: "I heard Abdullah Ibn Al-Abbas as saying: "A man asked the Messenger of Allah (peace and blessings be upon him) about Saba, whether it was a man, a woman, or a name of a land?"

The Prophet (peace be upon him) said: "Verily, he was a man to whom Allah gave ten sons. Six thereof inhabited the Yemen and 4 Sham (Syria). Those in Yemen were: Madhhaj, Al-Azd, Kindah, Al-Ash ariyun, Himyar and Anmar. And those that inhabited Syria were: Judham, Laghm, Amilah and Ghassan."

This means that the term Saba covers all these tribes. Among them also were At-Tababiah (Sing Tubba) in the Yemen. Their kings used to put crowns on as were done by the kings of Persia. The Arabs used to call whomsoever ruled over Hadramaut and Yemen "Tubba", as they used to call kings of Sham (Syria) and the Arab Peninsula "Caesar", and the ruler of Persia "Khusrau", the ruler of Egypt they called Firaun (Pharaoh), and the ruler of Abyssinia "Negus", and the ruler of India "Ptolemes", and Bilqis was from among the Himyar kings who ruled Yemen. They all lived in happiness with and Allah gave them an abundance of sustenance: fruits, plants, etc. and they were righteous people who followed the Straight Path. However, when they altered the Grace of Allah and denied it, they inevitably incurred to themselves and their peoples devastation and destruction.

Muhammad Ibn Ishaq narrating from Wahb Ibn Munabah said: "Allah sent them 13 Prophets. And, As-Sadi claimed that Allah the Almighty sent them 12,000 Prophets." Allah knows best!

When they replaced guidance with misguidance, prostrated themselves before the sun instead of Allah the Almighty, which took place during the era of Bilqis and her ancestors. Those continued until Allah sent floods released from the dam.
Allah said: "But they turned away (from the obedience of Allah), so We sent against them Sail Al-Arim (floods released from the dam), and We converted their two gardens into gardens producing bitter bad fruit, and tamarisks, and some few lote trees. Like this We punished them because they were ungrateful disbelievers. And never do We punish in such a way except those who are ungrateful."

Many scholars said that the Dam of Marab was built to keep water behind two great mountains. When the water sufficient, the people planted orchards and fruitful trees and many kinds of vegetables. It is said that the originator of the dam was Saba Ibn Yarub who changed the course of 70 valleys forcing them to pour out water therein. In addition, he forced the water to get out from 30 holes. However, he died before completing it. But the tribe of Himyar perfected it, and it was of the space of one square league. Thereupon, they lived in happiness and abundance. Qatada and others said that women (from among them) put baskets on their head, and the baskets would be filled with fresh, ripe fruits, and they said that the air they breathed was so clean and pure that neither flies, nor harmful germs were found in their land.

Allah said: "Indeed there was for Saba (Sheba) a sign in their dwelling place, two gardens on the right hand and on the left. And it was said to them: Eat of the provision of your Lord, and be grateful to Him. A fair land and an Oft-Forgiving Lord!" (Saba, 15) And remember when your Lord proclaimed: If you give thanks by accepting Faith and worship none but Allah), Allah will give you more of His Blessings, but if you are thankless, verily Allah's punishment is indeed severe." (Ibrahim, 7)

But, when they adorned others than Allah, and arrogantly dealt with His Grace, the stages of journey between them were easy in which they used to travel safely both by night and day, and asked Him to make the stages between their journeys longer and severer. Thus, they asked to turn the good into what is bad like the Children of Israel who asked Allah to turn Manna and quails into herbs, cucumbers, Fum (wheat or garlic), lentils and onions.

Thereupon, they were deprived that great blessing and comprehensive grace. Their land was destroyed and they themselves were scattered all over the globe.

Allah said: "But they turned away (from the obedience of Allah), so We sent against them Sail Al-Arim (flood released from the dam)."

Many scholars said: Allah the Almighty sent rats and mice on the bases of the dam, and when the people the rats, they sent cats to eat them up, but all that was in vain. The base of the dam became weak and finally the dam collapsed and the water drowned everything. Their good fruitful trees turned into as explained by Allah the Almighty bad ones: "And We converted their two gardens into gardens producing bitter bad fruit, and tamarisks. And some few lote-trees for they produce Nabk which is very few among the countless thorns they have."
Allah said: "Like this We punished them because they were ungrateful disbelievers.

And never do We punish in such a way except those who are ungrateful disbelievers). We only punish with this severe punishment those who disbelieved in Us, belied Our Messengers, disobeyed Our Orders, and violated Our Boundaries."

Allah said: "So We made them as tales in the land, and We dispersed them all totally. After the destruction of their gardens, properties and land, they had to move away. Thus, they scattered in different parts of the land as some of them moved to the Hejaz, and Khuzaah moved to Mecca. Some of them also moved to Al-Madinah Al-Munawwarah. They were the first to inhabit it.

Then, they were followed by three tribes from the Jews: the Banu Qainuqa, Banu Quraizah, and Banu An-Nadir. The Jews made coalitions with the Aus and Khazraj and lived there until the time of Prophet (peace and blessings be upon him)). Some of them, moved to Sham (Syria), and some afterwards converted to Christianity: Amilah, Ghassan, Bahra, Lukham, Judham, Taghlub, Tanukh, and others.

Muhammad Ibn Ishaq, in his The Prophet's Biography [Kitab As-Sirah], said that the first to leave the Yemen before the Sail Al-Arim (the flood released from the dam) was Amr Ibn Amir Al-Lukhami.

Lukham was the son of Adyi Ibn Al-Harith Ibn Murrah Ibn Azd Ibn Zaid Ibn Muha Ibn Amr Ibn Uraib Ibn Yashjub Ibn Zaid Ibn Kahlan Ibn Saba. It is said also by Ibn

Hisham: Lukham Ibn Adyi Ibn Amr Ibn Gharib Ibn Saba.

Ibn Ishaq said: "the reason behind his moving from Yemen as I was told by Abu Zaid Al-Ansari that he saw rats digging beneath the dam of Marab, which was used to keep the water behind, so he realized that the dam would soon break, so he wanted to move far away.

However, he tricked his people by ordering his youngest son to slap him on the face before the people. The son did what he was ordered to, and so Amr said: I would never live in a place where my youngest son slapped me on the face. And he offered his property to be sold.

The noblemen of the Yemen said: seize the opportunity of Amr's rage and buy all his property. Hence, he moved along with his children and their offspring. The Azd said: we never leave Amr Ibn Amir, so they sold their properties and accompanied him in his fleeing (without knowing his real intentions). They arrived at the land of Ak who fought against them and their war had its ups and downs.

Finally, they departed from the land of Ak and dispersed in the lands. Ibn Jafnah Ibn Amr Ibn Amir went to Sham (Syria), Al-Aus and Al-Khazraj went to Yathrib (Al-Madinah Al-Munawwarah), Khuzaah went to Marran, Azd As-Sarah went to As-Sarah, and Azd Amman went to Amman. Then Allah the Almighty sent the flood against the dam and so it collapsed. The Glorious Quran bears witness to this incident.

As-Sadi narrated the like and Muhammad Ibn Ishaq said that Amr Ibn Amir was a priest. Others said that his wife was Tarifah Bint Al-Khair Al-Himyariyah and that she was a priestess. She foretold the destruction of their country as if they saw an indication in those rats, so they did what they did, and Allah knows best!

His whole story was mentioned in the Exegesis on the authority of Ikriamh after Ibn Abu Hatim.

However, not all the people of Saba moved from the Yemen after the dam's destruction, some stayed there. Only the people of the Dam (Marab) went away and dispersed in the land. This is expressed in the Hadith mentioned earlier that was narrated by Abdullah Ibn Abbas, that the majority of the Yemenites did not move from the Yemen. Only 4 tribes left and 6 tribes stayed.
They continued to live there and they ruled the land until they were deprived of their own self-ruling for about 70 years by the army sent by the Negus under the command

of Abraha and Aryat. Then, it was regained by Saif Ibn Dhi Yazan Al-Himyari shortly before Prophet Muhammad's birth (peace and blessings be upon him).

Then, Allah's Prophet (peace be upon him) sent to the Yemen Ali Ibn Abu Talib and Khalid Ibn Al-Walid, then Abu Musa Al-Ashari and Muadh Ibn Jabal to invite the people to embrace Islam. Then, Al- Aswad Al-Ansi seized the Yemen and drove out the deputies of Allah's Messenger (peace and blessings be upon him). During the era of Abu Bakr As-Siddiq, Al-Aswad Al-Ansi was killed and the Muslims had the upper hand in the Yemen.

The Story of Uzair (Ezra) (9)

Allah the Almighty said:

Or like the one who passed by a town and it had tumbled over its roofs. He said: 'How will Allah ever bring it to life after its death?'

So Allah caused him to die for a hundred years, then brought him to life again. He said: 'How long was I dead?'

He (the man) said: 'Perhaps I was dead for a day or part of a day.'

The Angel said: 'You have been dead for a hundred years. Look at your food and your drink, they show no change and look at your donkey! And thus We have made of you a sign for the people. Look at the bones, how We bring them together and clothe them with flesh. When this was clearly shown to him, he said, I know (now) that Allah is Able to do all things.' (Al-Baqarah, 259)

The Jews say: 'Uzair (Ezra) is the son of Allah,' and the Christians say: 'the Messiah is the son of Allah.' That is their saying with their mouths, resembling the saying of those who disbelieved aforetime. Allah's Curse be on them how they are deluded away from the truth! (At-Taubah, 30)

Al-Hafiz Abu Al-Qasim Ibn Asakir said: He is Uzair Ibn Jarwah, or Ibn Suraiq Ibn Adiya Ibn Ayyub Ibn Darzna Ibn Ura Ibn Taqyi Ibn Usbu Ibn Finhas Ibn El-Azir Ibn Hamn Ibn Imran. Also, he is said to be Uzair Ibn Smkha. Some narrations state that his grave is located in Damascus. Then, Al-HafizIbn Asakir narrated on the authority of Abu Al-Qasim Al-Baghawi after Dawud Ibn Amr after Hibban Ibn Ali after Muhammad Ibn Kuraib after his father after Abdullah Ibn Abbas as saying: 'I do not know whether Tubba was a cursed one or not? And, I do not know whether Uzair was a Prophet or not?'

He narrated and said: Uzair a young boy among those captivated by Bikhtinassar. Bikhtinassar had erected an idol and ordered the people to prostrate themselves before it.

When Uzair was 40, Allah the Almighty granted him wisdom. And none was more knowledgeable than he, pertaining to the Torah, and he was mentioned with the train of Messengers and Prophets until his name was erased by Allah the Almighty when he asked about the Divine Decree. (This Hadith is weak and rejected) and Allah knows best! The divine decree is the al-qadr and the predestination. Al-qadr literally means "(divine) power."

Ishaq Ibn Bishr narrated after Sa'id after Abu Urubah after Qatadah after Al-Hasan after Abdullah Ibn Salam that Uzair was the man whom Allah caused to die for a hundred years, then raised him up again.

Ibn Ishaq Ibn Bishr said: I was told by Sa`id Ibn Bashir after Wahb Ibn Munabih: Uzair was a wise, pious worshipper. One day, he went out to look after some of his properties, when he finished he passed by a ruined place where he was scorched by the blazing sun. So, he entered that ruined place riding on his donkey. He got off the donkey holding two baskets, one full of figs and the other full of grapes. He sat down and brought out a bowl in which he squeezed the grapes and soaked the dried bread he had therein. He ate thereof and then slept on his back, relying his two legs against a wall and started to gaze at the ceiling of the house. He saw some decomposed bones and said: "Oh! How will Allah ever bring it to life after its death?" He did not doubt Allah's Omnipotence to do this, but he said it in exclamation.

Upon this, Allah the Almighty sent the Angel of Death who seized his soul, and thus Allah caused him to die for a hundred years. And, after one hundred years, Allah the Almighty sent to him an Angel who first created his heart to make him heedful, then, he created his two eyes to enable him to see and realize how Allah the Almighty revive the death. Then, the Angel continued to complete his creation once more while he was looking. The, he clothed his bones with flesh, skin and hair. Then, he breathed the soul into him. All this while he is looking and perfectly heedful. The Angel asked him saying: "How long did you remain (dead)?"

He (the man) said: Perhaps I was dead for a day or part of a day." That he was caused to die in the afternoon and then was given life again by the end of day while the sun was still in the sky. That is why he said: "or part of a day," i.e. not even a whole day. The Angel said: "Nay, you have been dead for a hundred years, look at your food and your drink," i.e. the dried bread and the squeezed grapes that did not alter or turn bad, they show no change, and the grapes and the figs did not change as well. As if he began to deny the matter by his heart, then the Angel said: "do you deny what I have said? Look at your donkey!"
He looked at his donkey and found his bones to be decomposed like dust. The Angel

called upon the donkey's bones and they answered his call and gathered together from all directions till he was made one whole again. While Uzair was looking and he clothed them with flesh, skin and hair.

Then, the Angel breathed life into it and it roused erecting his ears and head towards the sky thinking the Last Hour had come. That was stated in His Saying: "And look at your donkey! And thus We have made of you a sign for the people. Look at the bones, how We bring them together and clothe them with flesh."

And when this was clearly shown to him, he said, I know now that Allah is Able to do all things." Then he rode on his donkey back to his village where he was unfamiliar to the people and the people looked unfamiliar to him. Even he did not find his own house easily. When he reached the house, he found a crippled blind old woman at the age of one hundred twenty years old. She was a maid owned by him in the past and he left her while she was only twenty years old.

He asked her saying: "Is this the house of Uzair?" She said: "Yes, it is." She wept and said: "Today, no one ever remembers Uzair."

He told her that he was Uzair and Allah the Almighty caused me to die for one hundred years then He gave me life again."

She said: "Glory is to be to Allah! We lost Uzair one hundred years ago and never heard anything about him."

He said: "Verily, I am Uzair. She said: "Uzair was a man whose supplications were acceptable by Allah the Almighty, so invoke Allah to return my sight to me to look at you, so if you were Uzair, I would certainly know you."

Consequently, he invoked Allah the Almighty, then, he wiped over her eyes and they were recovered and took her by the hand and said: "Stand up by the Leave of Allah!" She stood up by the Leave of Allah. She looked at him and said: "I bear witness that you are Uzair." Then she set out for the Children of Israel in their meetings and gatherings and Uzair's son who was about one hundred and eighteen years old and his grandsons, and she called them saying: "This is Uzair who came back to you." They belied her, but she said: "I am so and so, your maid. He invoked Allah for me and He recovered my eyesight and legs. She added: he claims that Allah caused him to die for one hundred years and then He gave him life again."

The people rose up and went to look at him. His son said: "My father had a black mole between his shoulders". He disclosed his shoulders and they realized that he was Uzair. The Children of Israel said: "Uzair was the only one who committed the whole Torah to his heart and Bikhtinassar burnt it and nothing is left thereof but what the men can remember, so if you are the true Uzair write it down for us." His father, Surukha buried the Torah during that era of Bikhrinassar in a place known to nobody but Uzair. So he took them to that place and brought it out, but unfortunately, the papers were rotten and ruined. Consequently, he sat under the shade of a tree circulated by the Children of Israel and he renovated the Torah for them. At that time, two stars descended from the sky and entered into his mouth whereby he remembered the whole text of the Torah and thus renovated it to the Children of Israel. Thus, The Jews said: "Uzair (Ezra) is the son of Allah." (At-Taubah, 30) for the matter of the two stars, renovating the Torah and charging the affairs of the Children of Israel. He renovated the Torah for them in the land of As-Sawad. The town in which he died is said to be called "Sairabadh."

Abdullah Ibn Abbas (May Allah be pleased with him) said: "Thus he was as said by Allah the Almighty: And thus We have made of you a sign for the people," i.e. for the Children of Israel. That he was with his sons a young man among old people for he died when he was only forty and was revived on the same age and status. Abdullah Ibn Abbas said: he was resurrected after the time of Bikhtinassar. The same was related by Al-Hasan.

Was He a Prophet?

It is well known that Uzair was one of the Prophets sent to the Children of Israel. He came during the interval between Dawud and Suleiman, and Zakariya and Yahya. At his time, none from among the Children of Israel happened to memorize the Torah, Allah the Almighty inspired him to commit it to his heart and then he recited it to the Children of Israel. Wahb Ibn Munabih said: "Allah the Almighty ordered an Angel to descend with light to throw on Uzair. In doing this, he copied the Torah letter by letter until he was finished.

Ibn Asakir narrated on the authority of Abdullah Ibn Abbas (May Allah be pleased with him) that he asked Abdullah Ibn Salam about Allah's Statement: "The Jews say: 'Uzair (Ezra) is the son of Allah." (At-Taubah, 30) "Why did they say so?"

Ibn Salam mentioned his (Uzair's) writing down of the Torah out of his memory, and the saying of the Jews that Moses could not get them the Torah but in a book, and that Uzair got it without a book. Thereupon, some of them said: "Uzair (Ezra) is the son of Allah."

For this reason, many scholars said that there was a discontinuation pertaining to the transmission of the Torah at the time of Uzair. This is very likely if Uzair was not a Prophet which is adopted by Ata Ibn Abu Rabah and Al-Hasan Al-Basri, and that was narrated by Ishaq Ibn Bishr after Muqatil Ibn Suleiman after Ata Ibn Abu Rabah as saying: "That period witnessed 9 things: Bikhtinassar, Sanaa garden, Saba garden, Owners of the Ditch, Gasura, Owners of the Cave, Owners of the Elephant, Antioch, and Tubba."

Ishaq Ibn Bishr said: "I was told by Sa'id after Qatadah after Al-Hasan as saying: That period witnessed the issues of Uzair and Bikhtinassar." Moreover, it is transmitted in the Sahih Muslim that Allah's Messenger (peace and blessings be upon him) said: "I am most akin to the son of Mary among the whole of mankind and the Prophets are of different mothers, but of one religion, and no Prophet was raised between me and him (Jesus Christ)."

Wahb Ibn Munabih said: He was raised between Prophet Suleiman and Isa (Jesus) (peace be upon them). Ibn Asakir narrated after Anas Ibn Malik and Ata Ibn As-Sa'ib as saying: "Uzair was raised during the time of Moses Ibn Imran, and that he asked for permission to meet with Moses (Peace be upon him), but he refused because of his asking about the Divine Decree. He left while saying: 'to die a hundred times, is easier than tasting the humiliation for an hour.'"
As for what was narrated by Ibn Asakir and others on the authority of Ibn Abbas and others that he asked about the Divine Decree and so his name was erased from among

the names of the Prophets. It is a rejected as unauthentic Hadith that it is likely to be copied from the tales and stories that were invented by the Israelites.

Narrated Abdul Razzaq and Qutaibah Ibn Sa'id after Ja'far Ibn Suleiman after Abu Imran Al-Juni after Nuf Al-Bakali as saying: "Uzair said to his Lord: "O'Lord! You fashioned the creation, and You mislead whom You will and guide whom You will."

It was thus said to him: "Turn away from this!" But, he returned back. It was again said to him: "Turn away from this or your name as a Prophet would be wiped out. I am not to be questioned about My Doing, while they (all creatures) are brought into account pertaining to what they do."

At-Tirmidhi, narrated from the Hadith: Allah's Messenger (peace and blessings be upon him) said: "An ant had bitten a Prophet (one amongst the earlier Prophets) and he ordered that the colony of the ants should be burnt."

And Allah revealed to him: "Because of an ant's bite you have burnt a community from amongst the communities which sings *My Glory*."

The Story of Dhul Qarnain (10)

Allah the Almighty said:

And they ask you about Dhul-Qarnain. I shall recite to you something of his story. Verily, We established him in the earth, and We gave him the means of everything. So he followed a way. Until, when he reached the setting place of the sun, he found it setting in a spring of black muddy (or hot) water. And he found near it a people. We (Allah) said (by inspiration): "O Dhul-Qarnain! Either you punish them, or treat them with kindness." He said: "As for him (a disbeliever in the Oneness of Allah) who does wrong, we shall punish him, and then he will be brought back unto his Lord, Who will punish him with a terrible torment (Hell)."

But as for him who believes in Allah's Oneness and works righteousness he shall have the best reward, (Paradise), and we (Dhul-Qarnain) shall speak unto him mild words as instructions."

Then he followed another way. Until, when he came to the rising place of the sun, he found it rising on a people for whom We (Allah) had provided no shelter against the sun. So (it was)! And We knew all about him (Dhul-Qarnain). Then he followed (another) way. Until, when he reached between two mountains, he found, before (near) them (those two mountains), a people who scarcely understood a word. They said: "O Dhul-Qarnain! Verily Ya'juj and Ma'juj (Gog and Magog) are doing great mischief in the land. Shall we then pay you a tribute in order that you might erect a barrier between us and them?"

He said: "That (wealth, authority and power) in which my Lord had established me is better (than your tribute). So help me with strength (of men),] will erect between you and them a barrier. "Give me pieces (blocks) of iron;" then, when he had filled up the gap between the two mountain-cliffs, he said: "Blow!"
Then when he had made them (red as) fire, he said: "Bring me molten copper to pour over them." So they (Ya'juj and Ma'juj (Gog and Magog))) could not scale it or dig through it. Dhul- Qarnain) said: "This is a mercy from my Lord, but when the Promise of my Lord comes, He shall level it down to the ground. And the Promise of my Lord is ever true." (Al-Kahf, 83-98)

Was He a Prophet?

Allah the Almighty praised Dhul-Qarnain in the Glorious Quran for his justice. He ruled over the easts and wests and many regions where he subjected their peoples and ruled them with perfect justice. The most likely opinion is that he was a king.

Also, he was said to be a Prophet, or a Messenger. However, the most unlikely opinion thereof was that he was an *Angel*.

The latter was narrated after the Leader of the Faithful, Omar Ibn Al-Khattab (May Allah be pleased with him) who heard a man calling another saying: "O' Dhul-Qarnain! He (Omar) said: Shut up! Was it not enough with you to name yourselves after the Prophets, that you take names after those of the Angels?"

It is reported that Abdullah Ibn Amr said: "Dhul-Qarnain was a Prophet. Conversely, Abu Hurairah narrated that the Messenger of Allah (Peace be upon him) said: "I do not know whether Tubba was a cursed one or not? And, I do not know whether Hudud (the Prescribed Penalties) are expiatory for their people or not? And, I do not know whether Dhul-Qarnain was a Prophet or not?" (This Hadith is Odd and Strange)

In other narration, Ibn Abbas (May Allah be pleased with him) transmitted a report that goes to the saying that Dhul-Qarnain was a just king whose work was praised in Allah's Book (the Glorious Qur'an). He was made victorious; and Al-Khadir was his minister, leader of his army, and his consultant.

Al-Azraqi and others mentioned that Dhul-Qarnain embraced Islam at the hands of Ibrahim (Abraham) (Peace and blessings be upon him) and that he circumambulated around the Kabbah with him and his son, Ismail (Peace and blessings be upon them). Also, it was narrated after Ubaid Ibn Omair and his son, Abdullah and others: that

Dhul-Qarnain set out on foot to perform Pilgrimage. Upon hearing this, Ibrahim (Peace be upon him) welcomed him and invoked Allah for his sake and gave him advice as well. In addition, Allah the Almighty subjugated for Dhul-Qarnain the clouds to carry him wherever he wished. Allah knows best!

Why was he called "Dhul-Qarnain" (i.e. Owner of the two horns)?

This is a controversial issue, that there is not a definite known reason behind this. Some said: he had something on his head that looked like two horns. Wahb Ibn Munabih said: "He had 2 horns of brass on his head." (This interpretation is weak) Some scholars from among the People of the Book (Christians and Jews) said: "This is because he ruled over Persian and Roman territories." It was also said: "that he reached the first ray of the rising sun on the east and that on the west and he ruled over all that was in between." (The latter opinion is more likely true, which is the saying of Az-Zuhari)

Al-Hasan Al-Basri said: "He had two braids of hair that he used to fold up and thus was called 'Dhul-Qarnain'." And, Ishaq Ibn Bishr narrated that the grandfather of Omar Ibn Shuaib said: Dhul Qarnain, once, invited a tyrant king to the way of Allah. The king hit him on the head and broke one of his horns. Dhul-Qarnain invited him again and the tyrant broke the second horn. Thus, he was called "Dhul-Qarnain".

Narrated Ath-Thawri that 'Ali Ibn Abu Talib (May Allah be pleased with him) was once asked about Dhul-Qarnain. He replied saying: "He was a rightly-guided and pious man. He invited his people to Allah, but they hit him on his horn (side of the head) and he was killed."

Allah the Almighty resurrected him and he invited them again, again they hit him on his second horn and he was killed (for the second time). Allah the Almighty revived him and thus he was called "Dhul- Qarnain".

In other narrations, it was narrated by Abu At-Tufail after Ali Ibn Abu Talib that he said: "He was neither a Prophet, nor a Messenger, nor an Angel, but was a godly, pious worshipper."

What is his Name?

Scholars disagreed regarding his name. Az-Zubair Ibn Bakkar narrated after Abdullah Ibn, Abbas (May Allah be pleased with him): His name was Abdullah IbnAd-Dahhak Ibn Ma'd; or Mus'ab Ibn 'Abdullah Ibn Qinan Ibn Mansur Ibn 'Abdullah Ibn Al-Azd Ibn Ghauth Ibn Nabt Ibn Malik Ibn Zaid Ibn Kahlan Ibn Saba Ibn Qahtan.

It has been narrated in a Hadith that he was from the tribe of Himyar, and he was called the Philosopher for the excellence of his mentality. However, As-Suhaili said: "his name was Marzaban Ibn Marzabah." This was mentioned by Ibn Hisham who mentioned in another location that his name was: As-Sa'b Ibn Dhi Mara'id who was the grandfather of the Tababi'ah and it was him who gave the verdict to the benefit of Ibrahim (Peace be upon him) pertaining to the well of As-Sab.

It was said: He was Afridun Ibn Asfiyan who killed Ad-Dahhak. Al-Qass Ibn Saidah Al-Iyadi said in his famous sermon: "O'folk of Ayad Ibn As-Sab! Dhul- Qarnain ruled over the west and east, subjugated the Jinn and mankind, and he lived for 2,000 years. However, all this was just like a twinkle of the eye.

Ad- Daraqutni and Ibn Makula mentioned that his name was Hirmis, or Hirwis Ibn Qitun Ibn Rumi Ibn Lanti Ibn Kashaukhin Ibn Yunan Ibn Yafith Ibn Nuh (Noah (Peace be upon him)), and Allah knows best!

Ishaq Ibn Bishr narrated after Sa'id Ibn Bashir on the authority of Qatadah as saying: "Alexander was (called) Dhul-Qarnain, his father was the first Caesar, and he was from among the offspring of Sam Ibn Nuh (Noah (Peace be upon him))."

At this conjecture one should distinguish between two people who were called Dhul-Qarnain. The first is our pious Dhul-Qarnain while the second is Alexander Ibn Philips Ibn Masrim Ibn Hirmis Ibn Maitun Ibn Rumi Ibn Lanti Ibn Yunan Ibn Yafith Ibn Yunah Ibn Sharkhun Ibn Rumah Ibn Sharfat Ibn Tufil Ibn Rumi Ibn Al-As far Ibn Yaqz Ibn Al-'lis Ibn Ishaq Ibn Ibrahim (Peace be upon him).

This lineage was stated by Al-Hafiz Ibn Asakir in his Tarikh (History). Moreover, he was the Macedonian, Greek, Egyptian leader who established Alexandria and basing on whom the Romans set their Calendar. He came after the first Dhul-Qarnain with a very long time. This was 300 years before Jesus (Peace be upon him). His minister was the famous Philosopher Artatalis. Moreover, he was the one who killed Dara Ibn Dara, and subjugated the Persian kings and seized their lands.
We only drew the reader's attention to this because many people think that the two men called "Dhul-Qarnain" are me, which is a big mistake for there were great

differences between both. The first was a godly, pious, righteous worshipper of Allah the Almighty, and he was a just king whose minister was the pious man, Al-Khadlr. Moreover, some scholars stated that he was a Prophet as well. Whereas, the latter was a polytheist whose minister was a philosopher as mentioned earlier. In addition, the time elapsed between them both was more than two thousand years. Hence, none can miss the great differences and variance between both of them but an ignorant idiot who know nothing at all!

Allah's said: "And they ask you about Dhul-Qarnain." This was revealed because the people of Quraish asked the Jews of something about which they would ask the Prophet Muhammad (Peace be upon him) to test his knowledge.

The Jews told them: "Ask him about a man who traveled through the earth, and about some young men who set out and no one knew what happened to them?" Thereupon, Allah the Almighty revealed the stories of the Owners of the Cave and that of Dhul-Qarnain. Thus, He said: "Say: I shall recite to you something of his story," i.e., enough and sufficient news about him and his status. Then, He said: "Verily, We established him in the earth, and We gave him the means of everything", i.e., Allah the Almighty expanded his kingdom and provided him with what might enable him to gain what he wished to. Narrated Qutaibah that Ali Ibn Abu Talib was once asked about Dhul- Qarnain: "how could he reach the east and west?" Ali replied: "The clouds were subjugated for him, the means (of everything) were provided to him, and he was given extension pertaining to the light."

Narrated Abu Ishaq As-Subai'i after 'Amr Ibn 'Abdullah Al-Wada'i: "I heard Mu'awiyah as saying: four persons ruled over the earth: Suleiman Ibn Dawud the Prophet (Peace be upon them), Dhul-Qarnain, a man from the people of Hulwan, and another man. Someone said: "was it Al-Khadir?" Mu'awiyah said: "No!"

Az-Zubair Ibn Bakkar narrated that Sufyan Ath Thawri said: "I have come to know that four persons ruled over the whole earth: two of them were believers and the other two were disbelievers. The believing two were: Prophet Suleiman and Dhul-Qarnain. And, the disbelieving two were: Namrud and Bikhtinassar." The same was narrated by Sa' id Ibn Bashir.

Narrated Ishaq Ibn Bishr after Sa' id Ibn Abu 'Urubah after Qatadah after Al- Hasan as saying: "Dhul-Qarnain was a king after Namrud. He was a pious, righteous Muslim who traveled through the east and west. Allah the Almighty prolonged his life and granted him victory over the enemies and to get hold of their properties. He conquered the land, subjugated the people and traveled through the earth till he reached the east and west.

Allah the Almighty said: "And they ask you about Dhul-Qarnain. Say: I shall recite to you something of his story. Verily, We established him in the earth, and We gave him the means of everything, i.e. knowledge of seeking the means of fulfilling things."

Ibn Ishaq said: "Muqatil claimed that he used to conquer the lands and collect treasures, and used to offer the people two choices: whether they embrace his religion and follow him, or they be killed."

Ibn Abbas, Mujahid, Sa'id Ibn Jubair, Ikrimah, Ubaid Ibn Ya' la, As-Sadyi, Qatadah and Ad-Dahhak said: "and We gave him the means of everything, i.e. knowledge." Qatadah and Matar Al-Warraq said: "This means landmarks, locations, milestones and traces of the land."

Abdur Rahman Ibn laid Ibn Aslam said: "this means languages as he used not to conquer a people but he first speaks with them in their own language." The most possible and true explanation is that he knew all means through which he could fulfill his need or desire. As he used to take from every conquered region the provisions that enabled him to seize the next region, and so on.

Some scholars from among the People of the Book (Christians and Jews) mentioned that he spent 1600 years traveling through the land inviting people to the worship of Allah the Almighty Who has no partner in His Dominion. But, it seems that there is some exaggeration in specifying that lengthy period, and Allah knows best!

Allah's Statement "So he followed a way. Until, when he reached the setting place of the sun," i.e., he reached the place that no one can ever overpass, and he stood on the edge of the western ocean called Oqyanus wherein the islands called Al-Khalidat "The Eternal Ones". There, he could watch the setting of the sun. He found it setting in a spring of black muddy (or hot) water), i.e. the sea or ocean, as one who stands ashore sees the sun as if it rises from and sets in the sea. For this he said (he found it), i.e., as he thought.
Imam Ahmed narrated after Yazid Ibn Hamn after Al-Awwam Ibn Haushab as saying: "I was told by a freed-slave of Abdullah Ibn Amr after Abdullah as saying: Allah's Messenger (Peace and blessings be upon him) looked at the sun when it sat and said: "In Allah's blazing fire. Were it not for its prevention by Allah's Command,

it would burn all that is on earth." (This Hadith is very Strange and Odd and surely it is not an Authentic one)

Dhul-Qarnain Seeks the Eye of Life:

Ibn Asakir reported a lengthy narration in which Dhul-Qarnain had a friend from among the Angels called Ranaqil. Dhul-Qarnain asked him: "Do you know the place on earth called 'the Eye of Life'?"

The Angel described to him its location. Dhul-Qarnain set out seeking it appointing Al-Khadir as his harbinger. Al-Khadir came upon it in the land of darkness and he drank thereof. But, Dhul-Qarnain did not make it. However, Dhul-Qarnain met with a group of Angels in a palace there and he was given a stone. When he returned to his army, he asked the scholars who put it on a scale and put on the other one thousand stones of the like (weight and shape). However, the scale containing the first stone tilted.

He, then, asked Al-Khadir who put on the other scale a single stone and a handful of dry dust. Al-Khadir's scale tilted this time. He then commented saying: "This is like the son of Adam, he is never satisfied until he is buried (covered with dust)". Thereupon, the scholars prostrated themselves before him as a sign of respect and honor; and Allah knows best!

Then, Allah the Almighty informs us that Dhul-Qarnain gave verdicts pertaining to the people of that region. We (Allah) said (by inspiration): "O' Dhul-Qarnain! Either you punish them, or treat them with kindness."

He said: "As for him (a disbeliever, in the Oneness of Allah) who does wrong, we shall punish him, and then he will be brought back unto his Lord, Who will punish him with a terrible torment (Hell), i.e. he tastes the torment in this present life and in the Hereafter. He began with the torment of the present life for it is more difficult in the sight of the disbeliever. But as for him who believes (in Allah's Oneness) and works righteousness he shall have the best reward, (Paradise), and we (Dhul-Qarnain) shall speak unto him mild words (as instructions)) where he started with the reward of the Hereafter which is most important and he added thereto kindness, i.e. justice, knowledge and faith."

Allah the Almighty says: "Then he followed another way," i.e. he followed a way to return back from the west to the east. Some say that it took him twelve years to return to the east. Until, when he came to the rising place of the sun, he found it rising on a people for whom We (Allah) had provided no shelter against the sun, i.e. they do not have houses or any shelters to save them from the blazing sun. Some scholars say: "they used to resort to trenches dug in the earth to shelter then from the burning rays of the sun." Then, Allah the Almighty says: "So (it was)! And We knew all about him (Dhul-Qarnain)," i.e. Allah knows all about his affairs; He preserves and keeps him during his travels through the land from the west to the east and vice versa.

It was narrated after Ubaid Ibn Omair, his son Abdullah and others that Dhul-Qarnain performed Pilgrimage on foot. Upon hearing that, Ibrahim (Peace be upon him) met him and on their meeting he invoked Allah for his sake, and advised him. It was said also that he was brought a horse to ride, but he said: "I do not ride (on the back of horses) in a land wherein Prophet Ibrahim (Peace be upon him)." Hence, Allah the Almighty subjugated for him the clouds, and Ibrahim (Peace be upon him) gave him the glad tidings pertaining to this. The clouds used to carry him anywhere he wished for.

Allah the Almighty says: "then, he followed (another) way. Until, when he reached between two mountains, he found, before (near) them (those two mountains), a people who scarcely understood a word," i.e. they were ignorant. It was said that they were the Turk, 6 cousins of Gog and Magog. However, they told him that Gog and Magog wronged them and practiced mischief in their land. They offered him a tribute for that he builds a barrier (dam) preventing them from raiding over them. He refused to take the tribute they offered him finding sufficiency in that which Allah the Almighty has given him, so He said: "That (wealth, authority and power) in which my Lord had established me is better (than your tribute)."

Then, he asked them to bring him men and tools to erect the barrier between them. Gog and Magog could only reach them from that place located between two mountain-cliffs. The other paths were either vast seas, or high mountains. Consequently, he erected it using iron and molten copper. He put iron instead of bricks and molten copper instead of clay. Allah the Almighty commented: "so they (Gog and Magog) could not scale it) with escalators, (or dig through it) with axes or picks."

Dhul-Qarnain said: "This is a mercy from my Lord," i.e. Allah the Almighty decreed this to be a mercy from Him to His slaves that they no longer assaulted by Gog and Magog. "But when the Promise of my Lord comes," i.e. the time He decided for them (Gog and Magog) to demolish it and get out attacking mankind near the Last

Hour, He shall level it down to the ground, this will inevitably take place. As He says: "And the Promise of my Lord is ever true, and until, when Gog and Magog are let loose (from their barrier), and they swoop."

When mankind is resurrected from their graves, you shall see the eyes of the disbelievers fixedly staring in horror. (They will say): "Woe to us! We were indeed heedless of this nay, but we were Zalimun (polytheists and wrongdoers)." (Al-Anbiya', 96, 97)

Allah the Almighty says: "We shall leave them to surge like waves on one another," i.e., on the day Gog and Magog will come out, and the Trumpet will be blown, and We shall collect them (the creatures) all together. Narrated Abu Dawud At-Tyalisi after Ath-Thawri saying: "I have been informed that the first human being to shake hands (with someone else) was Dhul-Qarnain. Moreover, it was narrated on the authority of Ka'b Al-Ahbar that he said to Mu'awiyah: "Dhul-Qarnain on his death-bed told his mother, after his death, to prepare food and gather the women of the city and invite them to eat save anyone who lost any of her children (she should not eat thereof). The mother did as she asked, and none of them stretched a hand towards the food. She said: Glory be to Allah! Did you all lost children? They answered: By Allah! Yes we did. And, this was a great condolence for her."

Ishaq mentioned after Bishr Ibn Abdullah Ibn Ziyad after some of the People of the Book (Christians and Jews) the will of Dhul-Qarnain, an eloquent and lengthy advice, and that he died at the age of three thousand years. (This is very odd)

Ibn Asakir said: "I was informed that he lived for about 36 years. Others said: "he lived for 42 years and that he came 740 years after Dawud (David) (Peace be upon him). He came after Adam (Peace be upon him) with 5181 years and that his reign lasted for 16 years. But, that which he related is true as for the Macedonian Alexander and not our Dhul-Qarnain. He thus mixed the former with the latter and this is perfectly wrong. Among those who mixed them and declared both to be just one, was Imam Abdul Malik Ibn Hisham (Narrator of the Prophet's Biography), which was denied and rejected by Al-Hafiz Abu Al-Qasim As-Suhaili. He severely refuted his sayings and set clear boundaries between the two persons as mentioned earlier.

The Story of Gog and Magog (11)

Allah the Almighty said:

"They said: 'O'Dhul-Qarnain! Verily Ya'juj and Ma'juj (Gog and Magog) are doing great mischief in the land. Shall we then pay you a tribute in order that you might erect a barrier between us and them?' He said: 'That (wealth, authority and power) in which my Lord had established me is better (than your tribute). So help me with strength (of men), I will erect between you and them a barrier. Give me pieces (blocks) of iron,' then, when he had filled up the gap between the two mountain-cliffs, he said: 'Blow!' then when he had made them (red as) fire, he said: 'Bring me molten copper to pour over them.' So they (Ya 'juj and Ma 'juj (Gog and Magog)] could not scale it or dig through it. (Dhul-Qarnain) said: 'This is a mercy from my Lord, but when the Promise of my Lord comes, He shall level it down to the ground. And the Promise of my Lord is ever true." (Al-Kahf, 94-98)

And, until when Ya'juj and Ma'juj (Gog and Magog) are let loose (from their barrier), and they swoop down from every mound. (Al- Anbiya', 96)

No doubt, Gog and Magog are from among the children of Adam (Peace be upon him). In proof of this, comes the Hadith that is transmitted in the two Sahihs (Bukhari and Muslim) from Al-Amash, after Abu Salih, after Abu Sa'id Al-Khudri who narrated the Prophet (Peace and blessings be upon him) to have said: "Allah will say (on the Day of Resurrection): 'O'Adam!' Adam will reply: 'Labbaik wa Sa'daik, and all the good is in Your Hand.' Allah will say: 'Bring out the people of the fire.' Adam will say: 'O'Allah! How many are the people of the Fire?'

Allah will reply: 'from every one 1,000 take out 999.' At that time children will become hoary headed, every pregnant female will have a miscarriage, and one will see mankind as drunken, yet they will not be drunken, but dreadful will be the Wrath of Allah."

The Companions of the Prophet (peace be upon him) asked: "O'Allah's Messenger! Who is that 1 person from 1000?" He said: "Rejoice with glad tidings. One person will be from you and one 1000 will be from Gog and Magog." The Prophet (Peace be upon him) further said: "By Him in Whose Hands my life is, hope that you will be one-fourth of the people of Paradise." We shouted: "Allahu Akbar!" He added: "I hope that you will be one-third of the people of Paradise. We shouted: "Allahu Akbar!" He said: "I hope that you will be half of the people of Paradise." We shouted: "Allahu Akbar!"
He further said: "You (Muslims) (compared with non-Muslims) are like a black hair in the skin of a white ox or like a white hair in the skin of a black ox (i.e. your number is very small as compared with theirs)." (Al-Bukhari and Muslim)

This Hadith denotes the numerousness of their numbers and that they are a hundred-fold the number of all mankind. Moreover, they are from among the offspring of Noah (Peace be upon him) in particular for Allah the Almighty informs us in His Glorious Quran that Noah (Peace be upon him) invoked Him against the people of the earth saying:

"And Noah) said: 'My Lord! Leave not one of the disbelievers on the earth!'" (Nuh, 26) And, Allah the Almighty Himself says: "Then we saved him and those with him in the ship." (Al-Ankabut, 15)

This is in addition to the Hadith transmitted in Imam Ahmed's Musnad and the Sunan of Abu Dawud that mentioned: that there were 3 sons born to Noah (peace be upon him): Ham, Shem, and Japheth. Shem was the father of the Arabs; Ham was the father of the Sudan; and Japheth was the father of the Turk (not the people of Turkey). Moreover, Gog and Magog are just a part of the Turk from among the Mangols who were stronger and spread mischief in the land.

Some people claimed that Gog and Magog were created out of the semen of Adam (peace be upon him) that mixed with the earth and thus they were not from Eve. But, this claim which was held by Sheik Abu Zakariya An-Nawawi in his explanation of Sahih Muslim and by other scholars who declared it to be too weak. As, there is not any proof on this and moreover, it contradicts the obvious text of the Glorious Quran -mentioned earlier that all mankind of today are from the offspring of Noah (peace be upon him). In addition, some people claimed that they (Gog and Magog) are of different shapes and figures. Some are as tall as palm-trees, some are too short, and some take one of their ears as a bed and the other as a cover or blanket. However, all these claims are groundless and cannot stand the slightest refutation. But, the correct view is that they are from among the children of Adam (peace be upon him) and that they bear the same qualities and shapes.

The Messenger of Allah (peace and blessing be upon him) said: "Allah created Adam, making him 60 cubits tall. When He created him, He said to him, "Go and greet that group of angels, and listen to their reply, for it will be your greeting (salutation) and the greeting (salutations of your offspring. So, Adam said (to the angels), "As-Salamu Alaikum" (i.e. Peace be upon you).

The angels replied, "As-Salamu Alaika wa Rahmatu-l-lahi" (i.e. Peace and Allah's Mercy be upon you). Thus the angels added to Adam's salutation the expression, "Wa Rahmatu-l-lah." Any person who will enter Paradise will resemble Adam (in appearance and figure). People have been decreasing in stature since Adam's creation. This Hadith blocks the way before those who falsely claim things that are groundless.

A Very Important Question:

If it is said how does the previously-mentioned Hadith that was agreed upon denote that they will be treated as ransom for the Believers on the Day of Resurrection and that they will enter Hellfire, while no Messengers were sent to them and Allah the Almighty says: "And We never punish until We have sent a Messenger (to give warning)" (Al-Isra, 15)

The answer is that they will never be punished until they are given warning. Thereupon, if they were existing before the time of Prophet Muhammad (Peace be upon him) and Messengers were sent to them, thus, they were given warning. And, if no Messengers were sent to them, they would be treated as 'People of the Fitrah' and those to whom the Message of Islam did not reach or be conveyed. However, it is indicated by the Hadith transmitted by some of the Companions of the Prophet (Peace be upon him) that he said: "Those and the like will be tested on the pathways of the Resurrection: and whoever responds to the caller, he will enter Paradise. And, whoever refuses, he will enter the Fire."

However, testing them neither necessitates their salvation, nor contradicts with the saying that they will enter Hell-fire. For Allah the Almighty reveals to His Prophet (peace and blessings be upon him) what He wills of the Unseen, and hence, He informed him that they will be from among the people of Hell and that their nature denies the truth and submission thereto, as they do not respond to the caller until the Day of Judgment. This indicates that, they would be more stubborn in rejecting the truth if they were to come to know it in this present life. In the pathways of Resurrection, some of those who used to belie the truth in the present life will submit themselves to the truth.

Almighty Allah said: "And if you only could see when the Mujrimun (criminals, disbelievers, polytheists, sinners) shall hang their heads before their Lord (saying): "Our Lord! We have now seen and heard, so send us back (to the world), that we will do righteous good deeds. Verily! We now believe with certainty." (As-Sajdah, 12)

However, the Prophetic Hadith shows that the Prophet (Peace be upon him) invited them on the Night Journey to embrace Islam and they refused, this Hadith is an invented and fabricated one. The one who fabricated it was the liar, Amr Ibn As-Subh.

The (Dam) Barrier:

It was mentioned earlier that Dhul-Qarnain has built it out of iron and copper and elevated it to a very high point that is equal to the very lofty mountains. However, there is none on earth an equal to a building in terms of loftiness or benefiting to mankind. Imam Al-Bukhari transmitted in his Sahih the following Hadith saying: A man told the Prophet (peace and blessings be upon him) that he had seen the dam (of Gog and Magog).

The Prophet (peace and blessings be upon him) asked: "How did you find it?" the man said: "I found it like Al-Burd Al-Muhabbar (stripped garments)." The Prophet (peace and blessing be upon him) said: 'You have seen it like that."

In Ibn Jarir's exegesis of the Quran, a slight different narration was reported by Qatadah who said: "I was told that a man said: 'O'Allah's Messenger! I have seen the dam of Gog and Magog." The Prophet (peace be upon him) said: "describe it to me." The man said: "It looked like stripped garments, with red and black stripes." The Prophet (peace be upon him) said: "You have seen it."

It was mentioned that the Caliph, Al-Wathiq sent some messengers with messages to different kings to allow them travelling from one country to another till they reach the dam and stand on its reality. When they came back to the Caliph, they described it to him saying that it has a huge door with many locks. It is a very high and tight building and that the remnants of its building materials and tools are kept there in a tower. Also, there are still guards keeping an eye on it. They added that its location is on the northern-east side of the earth. It was also said that their land is very spacious and that they live on farming and hunting and that their numbers are countless.

How can we compromise between the Quranic Verse that reads: "So they (Ya'juj and Ma'juj (Gog and Magog)) could not scale it or dig through it." (Al-Kahf, 97) and the Prophetic Hadith that is transmitted by Imam Al-Bukhari and Imam Muslim on the authority of Mother of the Believers, Zainab Bint Jahsh (May Allah be pleased with her) as saying: That the Prophet (peace and blessings be upon him) once came to her in a state of fear and said: "None has the right to be worshipped but Allah. Woe unto the Arabs from a danger that has come near. An opening has been made in the wall of Gog and Magog like this, making a circle with his thumb and index finger." Zainab Bint lahsh said: "O'Allah's Messenger! Would we be destroyed even though there are pious persons among us?" He said: "Yes, when the evil persons will increase." And in another narration: The Prophet (peace be upon him) said: "Allah has made an opening in the wall of the Gog and Magog (people) like this, and he made with his hand (with the help of his fingers)." (Al-Bukhari and Muslim)

The answer is that this means one of two things: the first is that this is an indication of the opening of gates of evil and turmoil and hence, this is a mere example set for us. The second view considers this as narrating a concrete matter for His Statement, "So they (Ya'juj and Ma'juj (Gog and Magog)] could not scale it or dig through it," i.e., at their time for the sentence is in the past tense, the matter which does not contradict the possibility of its taking place in the future with the Permission of Allah the Almighty. But, as for the other Hadith that is narrated by Imam Ahmed in his Musnad that the Prophet (Peace be upon him) said: "Verily, Gog and Magog dig through the dam every day, until they could see the sun rays (through it), their leader would say: "Go back and you will finish it tomorrow. On the next day, they find it as strong as before. Till when their appointed term comes and Allah desires to send them against mankind, they dig it until they could see the sun rays (through it) and their leader says: "Go back and you will finish it tomorrow, if Allah wills!"

On the next day, they find it as they had left the day before and they dig through it and come against mankind. They will drink (every drop of water they pass by). The people will resort to strongholds. And, Gog and Magog will throw their arrows towards the sky. When they come back to them stained with what looks like blood, they will say: "We have defeated the people on earth and those in the heaven as well." Then, Allah the Almighty sends against them worms in their necks that kill them all. Allah's Messenger (peace and blessings be upon him) said: "By Whom in Whose Hand Muhammad's soul rests! Living creatures of the earth would go fat and be thankful due to eating their flesh and (drinking their) blood."

Imam Ahmed transmitted it also on the authority of Hasan Ibn Musa after Sufyan after Qatadah. At-Tirmidhi transmitted the same Hadith on the authority of Abu, Awanah after Qatadah, then he said: it is a Strange Hadith that reached us from none but this Chain of Transmission.

The Story of the People of the Cave (12)

Allah the Almighty said:

Do you think that the people of the Cave and the Inscription (the news or the names of the people of the Cave) were a wonder among Our Signs? Remember when the young men fled for refuge from their disbelieving folk to the Cave. They said: 'Our Lord! Bestow on us mercy from Yourself, and facilitate for us our affair in the right way!'

Therefore, We covered up their sense of hearing causing them to go in deep sleep in the Cave for a number of years. Then We raised them up from their sleep, that We might test which of the two parties was best at calculating the time period that they had tarried. We narrate unto you O'Muhammad (peace be upon him) their story with truth. Truly they were young men who believed in their Lord (Allah), and We increased them in guidance. And We made their hearts firm and strong with the light of Faith in Allah and bestowed upon them patience to bear the separation of their kith and kin and dwellings. When they stood up and said: "Our Lord is the Lord of the heavens and the earth, never shall we call upon any llah (god) other than Him, if we did, we should indeed have uttered an enormity in disbelief."

These our people have taken for worship alihah (gods) other than Him (Allah). Why do they not bring for them a clear authority? And who does more wrong than he who invents a lie against Allah. The young men said to one another: "And when you withdraw from them, and that which they worship, except Allah, then seek refuge in the Cave; your Lord will open a way for you from His Mercy and will make easy for you your affair (i.e. will give you what you will need of provision, dwelling). And you might have seen the sun, when it rose, declining to the right from their Cave, and when it set, turning away from them to the left, while they lay in the midst of the Cave. That is one of the Ayat (proofs, evidences, signs) of Allah. He whom Allah guides, he is the rightly guided, but he whom He sends astray, for him you will find no Wali (guiding friend) to lead him (to the Right Path). And you would have thought them awake, whereas they were asleep. And We turned them on their right and on their left sides, and their dog stretching forth his two forelegs at the entrance [of the Cave or in the space near to the entrance of the Cave (as a guard at the gate)]. Had you looked at them, you would certainly have turned back from them in flight, and would certainly have been filled with awe of them.

Likewise, We awakened them (from their long deep sleep) that they might question one another. A speaker from among them said: 'How long have you stayed (here)?' They said: 'We have stayed (perhaps) a day or part of a day.' They said: 'Your Lord (Alone) knows best how long you have stayed (here). So send one of you with this silver coin of yours to the town, and let him find out which is the good lawful food, and bring some of that to you. And let him be careful and let no man know of you. For, if they come to know of you, they will stone you (to death or abuse and harm you) or turn you back to their religion; and in that case you will never be successful.'

And thus We made their case known to the people, that they might know that the Promise of Allah is true, and that there can be no doubt about the Hour. Remember when the people of the city disputed among themselves about their case, they said: 'Construct a building over them, their Lord knows best about them.'

Then those who won their point said (most probably the disbelievers): 'We verily shall build a place of worship over them.' (Some) say they were three, the dog being the fourth among them; and (others) say they were five, the dog being the sixth, guessing at the unseen; (yet others) say they were seven, and the dog being the eighth. Say O'Muhammad (peace be upon him): 'My Lord knows best their number; none knows them but a few.' So debate not about their number except with the clear proof (which We have revealed to you).
And consult not any of them (people of the Scripture, the Jews and the Christians) about (the affair on the people of the Cave. And never say of anything, "I shall do such and such thing tomorrow." Except with the saying, "if Allah will!" And

remember your Lord when you forget and say: "It may be that my Lord guides me unto a nearer way of truth than this." And they stayed in their Cave 300 (solar) years, adding nine (for lunar years). Say: "Allah knows best how long they stayed. With Him is (the knowledge on the Unseen of the heavens and the earth. How clearly He sees, and hears everything! They have no Wali (Helper, Disposer of affairs, Protector) other than Him, and He makes none to share in His Decision and His Rule." (Al-Kahf, 9-26)

The reason behind the revelation of these verses and those relating the story of Dhul-Qarnain was cited by Muhammad Ibn Ishaq in his biography of the Prophet that the people of Quraish sent to the Jews asking them for things to test the Prophet (peace and blessings be upon him) with. The Jews said: ask him about a group of people who disappeared in the past and none has any knowledge about them, about a man who traveled through the land, and about Ar-Ruh (the Spirit).

Almighty Allah then revealed His Statement: "And they ask you (O'Muhammad (peace and blessings be upon him) concerning the Ruh (the Spirit); Say: "The Ruh (the Spirit) is one of the things, the knowledge of which is only with my Lord. And of knowledge, you (mankind) have been given only a little." (Al-Isra, 85) and,

"And they ask you about Dhul-Qarnain. Say O'Muhammad (peace be upon him): 'I shall recite to you something of his story.' (Al-Kahf, 83) and here He says: 'Do you think that the people of the Cave and 'Ar-Raqim' the Inscription (the news or the names of the people of the Cave) were a wonder among Our Signs?' i.e. they are not more amazing than what We have given you of the great news, astonishing signs and gigantic wonders. However, a cave is a hole in the mountain. Mentioned Shuaib Al-Jiba'i: their cave was called 'Haizam'. As for 'Ar-Raqim', Ibn Abbas (May Allah be pleased with him) said: I do not know what it means! Some scholars such as Ibn Jarir and others said: it is the record where their news and names are written thereafter. It was also said it is the name of the mountain their cave was in. However, many other things were said pertaining to this, but the knowledge thereof rests only with Allah the Almighty Who knows the best! Shu'aib Al-Jiba'i said: their dog was called 'Himran'.

The fact that the Jews knew about them nullifies the claim of some interpreters that they were after Jesus (Peace be upon him) and that they were Christians. However, it is clear that their people were idol-worshippers. Many interpreters and historians said that they lived during the lifetime of a king called 'Diqyanus' and that they were sons of some nobles or kings. They met on a feast day and saw the rituals their people were performing in worship of the idols. At this very moment, Allah removed the veils from their hearts and they realized that their people were wrong-doers. Consequently, they deserted the religion of their people and resorted to the worship of Allah Alone. It is also said that each one of them when guided by Allah to the True Religion, abandoned his people and they coincidentally gathered in one place.

Imam Muslim transmitted in his Sahih the following Prophetic Hadith which supports that meaning: "Abu Hurairah (May Allah be pleased with him) reported Allah's Messenger (Peace be upon him) as saying: Souls are troops collected together and those who familiarized with each other (in the heaven from where these come) would have affinity, with one another (in the world) and those amongst them who opposed each other (in the Heaven) would also be divergent (in the world)." That, they asked one another about their affair and hence, they agreed on deserting and abandoning their people and fleeing with their true religion.

Allah the Almighty said: "We narrate unto you O'Muhammad (peace and blessings be upon him) their story with truth. Truly they were young men who believed in their Lord (Allah), and We increased them in guidance. And We made their hearts firm and strong with the light of Faith in Allah and bestowed upon them patience to bear the separation from their people and dwellings. When they stood up and said: 'Our Lord is the Lord of the heavens and the earth, never shall we call upon any Ilah (god) other than Him. If we did, we should indeed have uttered an enormity in disbelief. These our people have taken for worship alihah (gods) other than Him (Allah). Why do they not bring for them a clear authority? And who does more wrong than he who invents a lie against Allah." (Al-Kahf, 13-15)

"Clear authority" here means obvious evidence or proof. And who does more wrong than he who invents a lie against Allah. The young men said to one another: "And when you withdraw from them, and that which they worship, except Allah," (Al-Kahf, 15, 16) i.e. when you deserted them and their idols that they used to worship others instead of Allah the Almighty.

And remember when Ibrahim (Abraham) said to his father and his people: "Verily, I am innocent of what you worship, except Him (i.e. Allah Alone I worship none), Who did create me, and verily He will guide me." (Az-Zukhruf, 26, 27)

Thus, some of these young men said as you did desert your people's religion, you should also desert them in body and figure so as to be safe from the possibility that their evil may touches you, then seek refuge in the Cave,. your Lord will open a way for you from His Mercy and will make easy for you your affair (i.e. will give you what you will need of provision, dwelling," (Al-Kahf, 16) i.e. Allah will draw on you His cover, protect you and reward you with the best of all rewards.

Then, Allah described the cave to which they resorted stating that its door is to the north saying: "And you might have seen the sun, when it rose, declining to the right from their Cave, and when it set, turning away from them to the left, i.e. the sun rises on the western side of their cave, then it declines to the right side thereof. And, when it sets its rays come towards the cave from its eastern side." Here, the wisdom is that the sun enters their cave on its rising and setting in order to refresh the air from time to time. While they lay in the midst of the Cave. That is one of the Ayat (proofs, evidences, signs) of Allah), i.e. their stay on this state for a very long period of time without eating and drinking is one of the Signs of Allah and a proof of His Magnificent Ability.

He whom Allah guides, he is the rightly guided, but he whom He sends astray, for him you will find no Wali (guiding friend) to lead him (to the Right Path). And you would have thought them awake, whereas they were asleep), for their eyes were open in order to be kept sound. And We turned them on their right and on their left sides, it was said: they used to be turned from one side to the other once every year. However, the number of the turnings is known only to Allah the Almighty Who knows best!

Allah the Almighty said: "And their dog stretching forth his two forelegs at the entrance of the Cave or in the space near to the entrance of the Cave (as a guard at the gate), i.e., their dog which accompanied them when they abandoned their people did not enter the cave with them, instead, it stayed at the entrance stretching forth his two forelegs thereat. This is for it was highly disciplined and also as a sign of honor to them because the angels do not enter a house in which there is a dog. Thus, the dog was blessed because he was in their company. However, many tales and narrations were invented with regard to the dog's name and color.

Scholars differed on the location of this cave. Some of them said it is in the land of Aylah (i.e. Jerusalem). Others said it is in the land of Ninawa. And others said it is in the Sham (Syrian territories) which is more proper and Allah knows best!

After Allah the Almighty gave us perfect and complete description of them and made us as seeing them, He said: "Had you looked at them, you would certainly have turned back from them in flight, and would certainly have been filled with awe of them," i.e., because of the dignity and loftiness of their appearance. The addressed her is not only Prophet Muhammad (peace and blessings be upon him) but also all mankind because it is a human nature to feel awe when seeing a magnificent or dignified thing. Then, Allah the Almighty awakened them (from their long deep sleep) after 309 years; then a speaker from among them said: "How long have you stayed (here)?" They said: "We have stayed (perhaps) a day or part of a day."

They said: "Your Lord (Alone) knows best how long you have stayed (here). So send one of you with this silver coin of yours to the town the coins they had were called "Dafsus". And let him find out which is the good lawful food, and bring some of that to you, i.e. to eat thereof. This is a sign of their piety and god-fearing. And let him be careful during entering that town and let no man know of you. For, if they come to know of you, they will stone you (to death or abuse and harm you) or turn you back to their religion; and in that case you will never be successful, i.e. if you turn back to their religion after you are saved by Allah the Almighty.

All this because they thought they slept a day or part of a day, and they did not imagine to have slept for more than three-hundred years. The period in which almost everything have changed and their generation passed away and other generations inhabited the land. Thus, when one of them went to the town to get the food, he feared that the people would recognize him, so he disguised. Instead, the town and its people found him to be a stranger and feared that he might be a spy or that he could harm them in any way. Some scholars said that he escaped from them. But, others said: he informed them with the news and took them to the cave to see his companions. When they approached the cave, he entered it and told his companions all about the period they spent sleeping in the cave and they confessed it to be the Divine Decree of Allah the Almighty. It was said: They went on sleeping; and others said: They all fell dead.

As for the people of the city, it was said that they could not see their place in the cave. Or, they could not enter the cave because of their cowardice, or feeling their lofty dignity. However, the people of the city disputed among themselves about their case, some of them said let us construct a building over them, i.e. block the cave's gate to prevent them from getting out or anyone from touching them with harm. But, those who won their point said that will be blessed because its nearness to these righteous and godly people. This was common in the previous eras and periods prior to Prophet Muhammad (peace and blessings be upon him). But, Islam rejects this deed. Building places of worship over the graves of anyone even if it is a Prophet. The Prophet (peace and blessings be upon him) said: "May Allah curse the Jews and Christians for they built the places of worship at the graves of their Prophets." The Prophet (peace and blessings be upon him) was warning (Muslims) against what the previous nations used to do with the graves of their pious people.

Allah the Almighty said: "And thus We made their case known to the people, that they might know that the Promise of Allah is true, and that there can be no doubt about the Hour," i.e. to let the people know that resurrection is true and that there can be no doubt about the Hour if they know that these young men slept for more than three hundred years then they were awaken unchanged. So, He Who kept them in this state all that period, is capable to resurrect and give life again to the dead bodies after they undergo decomposition. Really, the believers do not doubt this in the least: Verily, His Command, when He intends a thing, is only that He says to it, 'Be!' and it is!). (Ya-Sin, 82)

Allah said: "Some say they were three, the dog being the fourth among them, and others say they were five, the dog being the sixth, guessing at the unseen, yet others say they were seven, and the dog being the eighth, as Allah cited the dispute of the people among themselves as to their number. He cited three sayings, the first two He refuted and the third He stated, a matter which indicates that the third is the true one. However, Allah guided His Prophet (peace and blessings be upon him) to the good manners to be followed in such a case: that one should say: "Allah knows best!" For this, Allah the Almighty says: My Lord knows best their number.

His Statement: "None knows them but a few, from among the people. So debate not about their number except with the clear proof which We have revealed to you," i.e. an easy debate and do not exert yourself in such matters. "And consult not any of them (people of the Scripture Jews and Christians) about the affair of the people of the Cave," as He concealed their number from the very beginning of the story, saying: "Truly they were young men who believed in their Lord (Allah)." (Al-Kahf, 13)
So, if there was any benefit in mentioning their number, Allah the Almighty would certainly revealed it to us from the very beginning!

Allah the Almighty said: "And never say of anything, I shall do such and such thing tomorrow. Except with the saying, 'if Allah will!' And remember your Lord when you forget and say: 'It may be that my Lord guides me unto a nearer way of truth than this,'" this is a great and high moral lesson taught by Allah the Almighty that when anyone wishes to do something, he should say 'If Allah wills', because man cannot know what is hidden with Allah for tomorrow or for the future.

Abu Hurairah (May Allah be pleased with him) reported that Allah's Prophet (peace and blessings be upon him) said: "Suleiman lbn Dawud, the Messenger of Allah, said: 'I will have an intercourse with seventy wives during the night, and all of them will give birth to a male child who will fight in the cause of Allah. His companion or the angels said to him: Say, 'If Allah wills.' But he (Suleiman) did not say so, and he forgot it. And none of his wives gave birth to a child, but one who gave birth to a premature child."

Allah's Messenger (peace be upon him) said: "Had he said Insha'Allah (if Allah so willed), he would not have failed and his desire would have been materialized."

Allah the Almighty said: "And remember your Lord when you forget," for forgetting may be caused by the Devil, and remembering Allah gets the Devil out of one's heart and thus he remembers what he has forgotten.

And say: "It may be that my Lord guides me unto a nearer way of truth than this," i.e., if there were controversies and disputes about something, one should resort to Allah Who can facilitate it and make it so easy.

Allah the Almighty says: "And they stayed in their Cave three hundred (solar) years, adding nine," i.e., for lunar years. Say: "Allah knows best how long they stayed," i.e., if you are asked about this and you do not know exactly the answer, you should only attribute the matter to Allah the Almighty With Him is (the knowledge on the Unseen of the heavens and the earth, i.e., Allah knows the Unseen and gives knowledge thereof to none but Whom He wishes from among His creatures. How clearly He sees, and hears (everything)! i.e. He puts everything in its proper place with His Perfect Knowledge and Justice. Then, He says: "They have no Wali (Helper, Disposer of affairs, Protector) other than Him, and He makes none to share in His Decision and His Rule, i.e. He is the only Disposer of affairs and He is the King Who rules over everything.

The Story of the Believer and the Disbeliever (13)

Allah the Almighty said:

"And put forward to them the example of two men: unto one of them We had given them two gardens of grapes, and We had surrounded both with date palms; and had put between them green crops (cultivated fields). Each of those two gardens brought forth its produce, and failed not in the least therein, and We caused a spring to gush forth in the midst of them.

And he had property (or fruit) and he said to his companion: "I am much more than you in wealth, and stronger in respect of men." And he went into his garden in a state (of pride and disbelief). He was unjust to himself. He said: "I think not that this will ever perish. And I think not the Final Hour will ever come, and if indeed I am brought back to my Lord, (on the Day of Resurrection), I surely shall find better than this when I return to Him." His companion said to him: "Do you disbelieve in Him Who created you out of dust (i.e. like Adam), then out of Nutfah (mixed semen drops of male and female), then fashioned you into a man?" But as for my part, (I believe) that He is Allah, my Lord, and none shall I associate as partner with my Lord. "It was better for you to say, when you entered your garden: 'That which Allah wills will come to pass! There is no power but with Allah!' If you see me less than you in wealth, and children. It may be that my Lord will give me something better than your garden and will send on it Husban (torment, bolt) from the sky, then it will be a slippery earth.

Or the water thereof (of the gardens) becomes deep-sunken (underground) so that you will never be able to seek it." So his fruits were encircled (with ruin). And he remained clapping his hands (with sorrow) over what he had spent upon it, while it was all destroyed on its trellises, and he could only say: "Would that I had ascribed no partners to my Lord!" And he had no group of men to help him against Allah, nor could he defend (or save) himself. There (on the Day of Resurrection), Al-Walayah (protection, power, authority and kingdom) will be for Allah (Alone), the True God. He (Allah) is the Best for reward and the Best for the final end. (La ilaha illallah - none has the right to be worshipped but Allah). (Al-Kahf, 32-44)

Some scholars said that this is just an example that has not necessarily taken place in real life. But, the majority of scholars hold that it really took place and happened in life. His Statement: "And put forward to them the example," i.e. for the polytheists of Quraish as they wore their pride and showed arrogance to the weak and poor. This is like Allah's Statement that reads: "And put forward to them a similitude: the (story of the) dwellers of the town," [it is said that the town was Antioch (Antakiya)], when there came Messengers to them. (Ya-Sin, 13)

We know that one of the two men is a believer, while the other is a disbeliever. It is also known that one of them was very rich. The believer spent all his wealth in the Cause of Allah. Conversely, the disbeliever, though granted gardens and orchards, had diverted from Allah's Path. His two gardens contained grapes and date-palms surrounding his plants and grapes, along with overflowing rivers and water streams running everywhere along with his property. The fruits of his trees and plants were numerous and countless (only by Allah's Grace), and the sight of his gardens was very pleasant. However, the owner of the two gardens became very proud and dealt arrogantly with the believing man and said to him: "I am more than you in wealth and stronger in respect of men," i.e. I am better than you as you spent all your wealth in vain and you did not do as I did: "Buying gardens and orchards and investing the money therein to gain the profits later." You should have followed my very steps! And, he went into his garden while in a state (of pride and disbelief), unjust to himself), i.e. in a state that is not pleasing to Allah the Almighty (with pride and arrogance). And he said: "I think not that this will ever perish," that is because there is plenty of its plants and trees and if any of these were to perish, he would certainly (as he thought) get it replaced with a better ones. For he thought he has everything: plentiful water, countless fruits, and varieties of plants.

Then, the disbeliever said: "And I think not the Hour will ever come," as he put his perfect trust in the vain pleasures of this life of ours and belied the existence of the everlasting Hereafter. Then, he said: "And if indeed I am brought back to my Lord, (on the Day of Resurrection), I surely shall find better than this when I return to Him," i.e. if there is indeed a Hereafter and a Last Day, he will find there better than what he has been given in the present life. As he was deceived by what he was given and thought that Allah the Almighty granted him all these blessings because He loves him and favors him to other people. The same was said by Al-As Ibn Wa'il in His Saying: "Have you seen him who disbelieved in Our Ayat (the Quran and Our Prophet (peace be upon him) and said: "I shall certainly be given wealth and children [if I will be alive (again)]."

Has he known the Unseen or has he taken a covenant from the Most Gracious (Allah)? (Maryam, 77, 78). And, Almighty Allah says pertaining to the one He granted with blessings: "And truly, if We give him a taste of mercy from Us, after some adversity (severe poverty or disease, etc.) has touched him, he is sure to say: 'This is due to my (merit); I think not that the Hour will be established. But if I am brought back to my Lord, surely, here will be for me the best (wealth) with Him.'" (Fussilat, 50)

Then, We verily, will show to the disbelievers what they have done, and We shall make them taste a severe torment." (Fussilate, 50), and like Qarun said: "This has been given to me only because of the knowledge I possess." (Al-Qasas, 78) i.e. for Allah knows that I deserve it. But, Allah the Almighty said: "Did he not know that Allah had destroyed before him generations, men who were stronger than him in might and greater in the amount (of riches) they had collected? But the Mujrimun (criminals, disbelievers, polytheists, sinners) will not be questioned of their sins (because Allah knows them well, so they will be punished without being called to account)." (Al-Qasas, 78)

And, Allah the Almighty said: "And it is not your wealth, nor your children that bring you nearer to Us (i.e. please Allah), but only he who believes (in the Islamic Monotheism), and does righteous deeds (will please Us), as for such, there will be twofold reward for what they did, and they will reside in the high dwellings (Paradise) in peace and security) (Saba, 37) and, Do they think that in wealth and children with which We enlarge them. We hasten unto them with good things. Nay, [it is a Fitnah (trial) in this worldly life so that they will have no share of good things in the Hereafter] but they perceive not." (Al-Mu'minun, 55, 56)

When this ignorant was deluded by what he has been given in this present life, he denied the Hereafter and claimed that if it is to be there, he would find that which is better than what he was first given. When his companion (the believing man) heard him saying so, he said to him: "Do you disbelieve in Him Who created you out of dust (i.e. your father Adam), then out of Nutfah (mixed semen drops of male and female), then fashioned you into a man?" i.e. do you disbelieve in the Day of

Resurrection while you know that He, Allah, is Him Who created you out of dust, then out of Nutfah, then fashioned you in stages till you became a sound and well-erected man with hearing, sight, understanding and organs you transgress with! Then, how could you deny the Resurrection while you know that Allah is capable of creating you out of nothingness. "But as for my part, (I believe) that He is Allah, my Lord," i.e. I believe in other than what you believe in or even think of. As "(I believe) that He is Allah, my Lord, and none shall I associate as partner with my Lord," i.e. I do not worship other than Him and I believe in that He will resurrect the dead and gather the scattered and rotten bones together, and I know that there is no partner with Allah in His Dominion or creation, and that there is no god but Him."

Then, he guided him towards what should have been said upon entering the garden saying: "It was better for you to say, when you entered your garden: 'That which Allah wills (will come to pass)! There is no power but with Allah!'" for it is better for anyone who becomes admirer of any of his wealth, household, children or status, he should say these words: (That which Allah wills (will come to pass)! There is no power but with Allah!).

Then, the believer said to the disbeliever: "If you see me less than you in wealth, and children. It may be that my Lord will give me something better than your garden," i.e. in the Hereafter. "And will send on it Husban (torment, bolt) from the sky," i.e. torment or heavy rain that uproots its trees and plants, "then it will be a slippery earth," i.e. soft dust that does not grow plants or anything. "Or the water thereof (of the gardens) becomes deep-sunken (underground)" that is opposite to the overflowing water, "so that you will never be able to seek it," i.e. you will never be able to restore or regain it. Then, Allah the Almighty says: "So his fruits were encircled (with ruin)," i.e. all his fruits and plants were ruined and totally destroyed. "And he remained clapping his hands (with sorrow) over what he had spent upon it, while it was all destroyed on its trellises," i.e. destroyed and ruined. That was really against his hopes and wishes as he previously said: "I think not that this will ever perish." So, he regretted his previous acts and sayings that declared him as a disbeliever in Allah the Almighty and he could only say: "Would that I had ascribed no partners to my Lord!"

Allah the Almighty says: "And he had no group of men to help him against Allah, nor could he defend (or save) himself," i.e. he could neither be helped by others, or even help himself. This is as the Statement of Allah that reads: "Then he will have no power, nor any helper."
(At-Tariq, 10)

His Saying: "There (on the Day of Resurrection), Al- Walayah (protection, power, authority and kingdom) will be for Allah (Alone), the True God), i.e. the irrefutable judgment and irresistible ruling on this and on all conditions will be for Allah the Almighty Alone. (He (Allah) is the Best for reward and the Best for the final end," i.e. trading with Allah is better than anything else as He gives the best of all rewards and with Him rests the best of all ends and goals. Finally, this story denotes three things:

(a) One should not sell himself out to the luxuries of this present life of ours and should not be deluded thereof. Moreover, one should trust what is in Allah's Hand more than what is in his own hand. One should put his entire trust in Allah Alone. Obedience of Allah should be one's first and final goal. Anyone who prefers anything to Allah and His obedience surely will be tormented thereof.

(b)   One should whole-heartedly accept the advice of his compassionate brother, as in rejecting his counselor advice there rests complete destruction and perfect ruin.

(c)   Regretting goes in vain if the Divine Decree is already done.

The Story of People of the Garden (14)

Allah the Almighty said:

"Verily, We have tried them as We tried the people of the garden, when they swore to pluck the fruits of the (garden) in the morning. Without saying: 'Insha'Allah (If Allah wills).' Then there passed by on the (garden) a visitation (fire) from your Lord at night and burnt it while they were asleep. So the (garden) became black by the morning, like a pitch dark night (in complete ruins). Then they called out one to another as soon as the morning broke. Saying: 'Go to your tilth in the morning, if you would pluck the fruits.'

So they departed, conversing in secret low tones (saying): No Miskin (poor man) shall enter upon you into it today. And they went in the morning with strong intention, thinking that they have power (to prevent the poor taking anything of the fruits therefrom). But when they saw the (garden), they said: 'Verily, we have gone astray.' (Then they said): 'Nay! Indeed we are deprived of (the fruits)!' The best among them said: 'did I not tell you: why say you not: Insha'Allah (If Allah wills).' They said: 'Glory to Our Lord! Verily, we have been Zalimun (wrong-doers).' Then they turned one against another, blaming. They said: 'Woe to us! Verily, we were Taghun (transgressors and disobedient). We hope that our Lord will give us in exchange a better (garden) than this. Truly, we turn to our Lord (wishing for good that He may forgive our sins and reward us in the Hereafter). Such is the punishment (in this life), but truly the punishment of the Hereafter is greater if they but knew.'" (Al-Qalam, 17- 33)

This is an example set by Allah the Almighty for the polytheists of Quraish as He favored them with sending the honorable and great Prophet, Muhammad (Peace and blessings be upon him), but they belied him and rejected what he had brought them. Almighty Allah, says: "Have you not seen those who have changed the Blessings of Allah into disbelief (by denying Prophet Muhammad and his Message of Islam), and caused their people to dwell in the house of destruction? Hell, in which they will burn, and what an evil place to settle in!" (Ibrahim, 28, 29)

Ibn Abbas (May Allah be pleased with him) said: "They are the polytheists of Quraish whom were likened to the people of the garden that contained various fruits and plants that were ripe and the time of their harvesting has come. Thus, He, Glory be His, says: 'when they went secretly to pluck the fruits of the (garden),'
i.e. to harvest it in the morning in order not to be seen by either a poor, or a needy and be forced to donate to or give them any of its fruits. So, they swore to this without saying 'If Allah wills.' Consequently, Allah the Almighty disabled them and sent over their garden fire that burnt it and left nothing thereof. He, Glory be His, says: 'Then, there passed by on the (garden) a visitation (fire) from your Lord at night and burnt it while they were asleep. So the (garden) became black by the morning, like a pitch dark night (in complete ruins)."

Allah the Almighty says: "Then they called out one to another as soon as the morning broke," i.e. they got up in the morning and they called out one to another saying: "Go to your tilth in the morning, if you would pluck the fruits," i.e. go early to your garden and pluck the fruits before the poor and needy persons come to ask you for charity. The story goes: "So they departed, conversing in secret low tones," i.e. talking one to another in low tones saying: "No Miskin (poor man) shall enter upon you into it today," i.e. they agreed upon that and made mutual consultations thereto. The story goes on: "And they went in the morning with strong intention, thinking that they have power (to prevent the poor taking anything of the fruits therefrom)," i.e. they went forth with seriousness, power and strong bad intention.

Ikrimah and Ash-Shu`abi said: "And they went in the morning with strong intention," i.e. rage and bad intention against the poor. But when they saw the (garden), i.e. when they reached their garden and found what had happened to it, upon this, they said: "Verily, we have gone astray," i.e. we have lost our way to our own garden, then they said: "Nay! Indeed we are deprived of (the fruits)!" i.e. we have been punished because of our bad intentions and were deprived of the blessing of our tilth.

And, the best among them said: "Did I not tell you: why say you not: Insha'Allah (If

Allah wills), it was said: To say a good word instead of what you have intended."

Ibn Abbas (May Allah be pleased with him), Mujahid and others said: "He was the best and the most moderate and just one among them all." They said: "Glory to Our Lord! Verily, we have been Zalimun (wrong-doers)." Then they turned one against another, blaming. They said: "Woe to us! Verily, we were Taghun (transgressors and disobedient)," they regretted and showed sorrow when both could do them nothing, and they confessed their sinful deed after they had been punished and all that went in vain.

It was said that they were brothers and they inherited that garden from their late father who used to give much and much in charity. But, when they possessed the garden they denied the acting of their late father and intended to deprive the poor of its fruits. Thereupon, Allah the Almighty punished them and gave them the severest of penalties. For this, Allah the Almighty commanded that charity must be taken out of fruits and it is preferably to be paid on the day of harvesting. He says: "Eat of their fruit when they ripen, but pay the due thereof (its Zakah, according to Allah's Orders $1/10^{th}$ or $1/20^{th}$) on the day of its harvest." (Al-An'am, 141)

It was said that they were from the Yemen, from a town called "Darwan". It was also said: They were from Abyssinia. Allah knows best!

Allah the Almighty says: "Such is the punishment," i.e. like this We punish those who disobey Our Command and does not show kindness to the needy from among Our creatures. But truly the punishment of the Hereafter is greater than that of the present life if they but knew."

This story resembles Allah's Saying: "And Allah puts forward the example of a township that dwelt secure and well-content: its provision coming to it in abundance from every place, but it (its people) denied the Favors of Allah (with ungratefulness). So Allah made it taste extreme of hunger (famine) and fear, because of that evil, i.e. denying Prophet Muhammad (Peace be upon him), which its people used to do. And verily, there had come unto them a Messenger (peace be upon him) from among themselves, but they denied him, so the torment overtook them while they were Zalimun (polytheists and wrong-doers)." (An-Nahl, 112, 113) It was said that this example was of the people of Mecca set for themselves and verily, there is no contradiction in this. Allah knows best!

The Story of the Sabbath-Breakers (15)

Allah the Almighty said:

"And ask them O'Muhammad (peace and blessings be upon him) about the town that was by the sea. Its people transgressed in the matter of the Sabbath (Saturday): 'when their fish came to them openly on the Sabbath day, and did not come to them on the day they had no Sabbath.' Thus We made a trial of them, for they used to rebel against Allah's Command (disobey Allah). And when a community among them said: 'Why do you preach to a people whom Allah is about to destroy or to punish with severe torment?' (The preachers) said: 'in order to be free from guilt before your Lord (Allah), and perhaps they may fear Allah.' So when they forgot the remindings that had been given to them, We rescued those who forbade evil, but We seized those who did wrong with a severe torment because they used to rebel against Allah's Command (disobey Allah). So when they exceeded the limits of what they were prohibited, We said to them: 'Be you monkeys, despised and rejected.'" (Al-A' rat, 163-166)

And, "And indeed you knew those amongst you who transgressed in the matter of the Sabbath (Saturday). We said to them: 'Be you monkeys, despised and rejected.' So We made the punishment an example to their own and also to succeeding generations and a lesson to those who are Al-Muttaqun (the pious)."
(Al-Baqarah, 65, 66)

Abdullah Ibn 'Abbas, Mujahid,' Ikrimah, Qatadah, As-Sadiy and others said: "they were the people of Aylah." Ibn Abbas (May Allah be pleased with him) added: "it was located between Median and At-Tur." They said: "the people of Aylah were adhering attentively to the teachings of the Torah and the prohibition of the Sabbath at that time (the prohibition of fishing on Saturdays)." Amazingly, the fish used to expose itself openly on Saturdays and disappear on the other days of the week, when their fish came to them openly on the Sabbath day, and did not come to them on the day they had no Sabbath. Almighty Allah says: "Thus We made a trial of them," i.e. We test them through sending great numbers of fish on the Sabbath.

They used to rebel against Allah's Command (disobey Allah). When they saw this, they made a trick to catch the fish on the Sabbath. They fixed their fishing nets and ropes and excavated streams allowing the sea water to run through and the fish to get in but never go back to the sea. They made all this on Friday, in preparation for the coming of the fish on Saturday. And thus, the fish came on the supposedly-peaceful day (knowing not what has been prepared against them). They were caught in the nets, ropes and artificial streams. When the Saturday came to an end, the people of Aylah were present to take their fat catch. Consequently, Allah the Almighty was angry with them and He cursed them because of their trickery and deception. When this was done by a group thereof, the rest who did not participate in their sinful acting were divided into two sects: a sect that rejected their acting and trickery against the Law and Command of Allah the Almighty at that time. The second sect did not reject or forbid them, rather they disapproved of the reaction of the sect that forbade the sinful ones saying: "Why do you preach to a people whom Allah is about to destroy or to punish with a severe torment?" i.e. what is the gain in preaching to a people whom will inevitably be punished by Allah the Almighty? But, the second sect (the preachers) replied saying: "In order to be free from guilt before your Lord (Allah0," i.e. as we are commanded by Him to enjoin what is good and forbid what is evil; thus, we observe this for our fear of His Torment. "And perhaps they may fear Allah," i.e. perhaps those who made these sins may repent to Allah and regret what they have done and thus be saved from the punishment of Allah and that He forgives them all. Allah the Almighty says: "So when they forgot the reminders that had been given to them," i.e. were heedless towards the godly preachers. We rescued those who forbade evil," i.e. the preaching sect, but "We seized those who did wrong," i.e. doers of the sinful deed, with a severe torment, i.e. a painful punishment, (because they used to rebel against Allah's Command (disobey Allah)). Then, Allah explained the torment that befell them saying, "So when they exceeded the limits of what they were prohibited, We said to them: Be you monkeys, despised and rejected."

Here, the point is that Allah the Almighty informed us that He destroyed the wrong-doers, saved the preaching believers and left the believers who did not practice enjoining the good and forbidding the evil. Scholars disputed regarding the third group. Some said they were granted salvation. And others said that they were destroyed with the wrong-doers. But, the first view is the accepted one by the well-versed scholars, including Ibn Abbas head of the interpreters - who referred to this opinion on a debate with his master lkrimah who upon the victory of Ibn Abbas - granted him a valuable garment as a reward.

It should be noted here that the third group were not mentioned with those given salvation even though they despised the sinful deed, with their hearts, because they should have compelled their organs (hand or tongue) to act thereupon and declare their rejection of the wrong-doers' act. So, they were saved with the preachers because they themselves did not commit the sinful deed, rather they rejected it with their hearts.

Narrated Abdur Razzaq after Juraij after a man (whose name is not known) after Ikrimah after Ibn Abbas; and Malik transmitted from Ibn Ruman, Shaiban, Qatadah and Ata Al-Kharasani what means: "Those who committed the sinful deed were abandoned by the rest of the people of the town." Some of them declared their rejection and denial of their deed. They did not listen to the preachers. Afterwards, they used to stay the night apart from the rest of the people of the town and there were doors or barriers between them and the rest of the people who were anticipating the befalling of punishment over them. One day, their doors did not open till the noon. The people got anxious and sent one of them to see what happened to them from above the barrier. When he looked he found them turned into monkeys with tails, shouting. They opened the doors (barrier) and the monkeys recognized their relatives while their relatives could not recognize them. Thereupon, the preachers said: "Did not we forbid you from doing this?" The monkeys made a sign with their heads denoting: "Yes." Then, Abdullah Ibn Abbas (May Allah be pleased with him) wept and said: "verily, we see many wrong-doings which we do not reject or deny or even make a comment!"

Narrated Al-Ufi after Ibn Abbas (May Allah be pleased with him) saying: "the young men of the town were turned into monkeys, while the old men into pigs." Moreover, Ibn Abu Hatim narrated from Muja-Qid after Ibn Abbas his saying: "they did not live long and they left no offspring." Also, Adpahhaq narrated from Ibn Abbas (May Allah be pleased with him): "no monster has lived more than three days." In addition, they did not eat, drink or leave offspring.

Narrated Ibn Abu Hatim and Ibn Jarir after Ibn Abu Nujaih from Mujahid his saying:

"only their hearts and not their figures were turned into monkeys and pigs." This is just like His Statement that reads: "The likeness of those who were entrusted with the (obligation of the) Taurat (Torah) (i.e. to obey its commandments and practice its laws), but who subsequently failed in those (obligations), is as the likeness of a donkey which carries huge burdens of books (but understands nothing from them)." (Al-Jumuah, 5) But, this view seems to be very strange and it contradicts the apparent meaning of the Glorious Quran and the concession of the earlier scholars and

The Story of Luqman (16)

Allah the Almighty said:

"And indeed We bestowed upon Luqman Al-Hikmah (wisdom and religious understanding) saying: 'Give thanks to Allah.' And whoever gives thanks, he gives thanks for (the good of) his own self. And whoever is unthankful, then verily, Allah is All-Rich (Free of all needs), Worthy of all praise. And (remember) when Luqman said to his son when he was advising him: "O my son! Join not in worship others with Allah. Verily, joining others in worship with Allah is a great Zulm (wrong) indeed. And We have enjoined on man (to be dutiful and good) to his parents. His mother bore him in weakness and hardship upon weakness and hardship, and his weaning is in two years, give thanks to Me and to your parents. Unto Me is the final destination. But if they (both) strive with you to make you join in worship with Me others that of which you have no knowledge, then obey them not; but behave with them in the world kindly, and follow the path of him who turns to Me in repentance and in obedience. Then to Me will be your return, and I shall tell you what you used to do. "O'my son! If it be (anything) equal to the weight of a grain of mustard seed, and though it be in a rock, or in the heavens or in the earth, Allah will bring it forth. Verily, Allah is Subtle (in bringing out that grain), Well-Aware (of its place). O my son!"

So, Luqman started by advising him to worship Allah Alone, and not to associate anything with Him. Then he warned him:

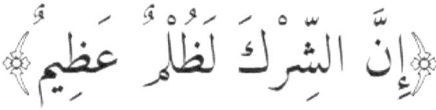

(Verily, joining others in worship with Allah is a great Zulm (wrong) indeed.) meaning, it is the greatest wrong.

Aqim-As-Salat (perform As-Salat), enjoin (on people) Al-Maruf (Islamic Monotheism and all that is good), and forbid (people) from Al-Munkar (i.e. disbelief in the Oneness of Allah, polytheists of all kinds and all that is evil and bad), and bear with patience whatever befalls you. Verily, these are some of the important commandments (ordered by Allah with no exemption). "And turn not your face away from men with pride, nor walk in insolence through the earth. Verily, Allah likes not any arrogant boaster."

"And be moderate (or show no insolence) in your walking and lower your voice. Verily, the harshest of all voices is the braying of the donkey." (Luqman, 12-19)

He is Luqman Ibn Anqa Ibn Sadun. Or, as stated by As-Suhaili from Ibn Jarir and Al-Qutaibi that he is Luqman Ibn Tharan who was from among the people of Aylah (Jerusalem).

He was a pious man who exerted himself in worship and who was blessed with wisdom. Also, it is said that he was a judge during the lifetime of Prophet Dawud (Peace be upon him). And, Allah knows best.

Narrated Sufyan Ath-Thawri from Al-Ash'ath after 'Ikrimah on the authority of Ibn 'Abbas (May Allah be pleased with him) as saying: He was an Ethiopian slave who worked as a carpenter. Qatadah narrated from' Abdullah Ibn Az-Zubair as saying: I asked Jabir Ibn Abdullah about Luqman. He said: "He was short with a flat nose. He was from Nubia."

Narrated Yahia Ibn Sa'id Al-Ansari after Sa'id Ibn Al-Musayib his saying: Luqman belonged to the black men of Egypt. He had thick lips and Allah the Almighty granted him wisdom but not Prophethood. Al-Awza'i said: "I was told by Abdur Rahman Ibn Harmalah that a black man came to Sa'id Ibn Al-Musayib asking him for charity. Sa'id said: do not feel distressed for your black color because there were from among the best of all people three blackmen: Bilal Ibn Rabah, Mahja (the freed-slave of Omar Ibn Al-Khattab), and Luqman, the wise who was black, from Nubia and whose lips were thick."

Narrated Al-Amash after Mujahid: Luqman was a black huge slave, thick-lipped, and cracked footed. Omar Ibn Qais said: "Luqman was a black slave, thick-lipped and cracked-footed." It happened while he was preaching some people, a man came to him and said: "are you the one who used to look after the sheep with me at such and such place?" Luqman said: "yes, I am!" The man said: "then, what made you of that position?" Luqman said: "telling the truth and keeping silent regarding what does not concern me." (This Hadith was narrated by Ibn Jarir after lbn Hamid after Al-Hakam)

Ibn Abu Hatim said: "I was told by Abu Zarah that he was told by Safwan after Al-Walid after Abdur Rahman Ibn Abu Yazid Ibn Jabir who said: "Allah the Almighty raised Luqman's status for his wisdom." A man used to know him saw him and said: "Aren't you the slave of so and so who used to look after my sheep not so long in the past?" Luqman said: "yes!"

The man said: "What raised you to this high state I see?" Luqman said: "the Divine Decree, repaying the trust, telling the truth and discarding what does not concern me."

Narrated Ibn Wahb: I was told by Abdullah Ibn Ayyash Al-Fityani after Omar, the freed slave of Afrah as saying: "A man came to Luqman, the wise and asked: 'Are you Luqman? Are you the slave of so and so?' He said: 'Yes!' The man said: 'You are the black shepherd!' Luqman said: "As for my black color, it is obviously apparent, so what makes you so astonished?' The man said: 'You became frequently visited by the people who pleasingly accept your judgments!' Luqman said: 'O'cousin! If you do what I am telling you, you will be like this.' The man said: 'What is it?'

Luqman said: 'Lowering my gaze, watching my tongue, eating what is lawful, keeping my chastity, undertaking my promises, fulfilling my commitments, being hospitable to guests, respecting my neighbors, and discarding what does not concern me. All these made me the one you are looking at.'"

One day Abu Ad-Darda mentioned Luqman the wise and said: "He was not granted wisdom because of wealth, children, lineage, or given habits, but he was self-restrained, taciturn, deep-thinking, and he never slept during the day. In addition, no one has ever seen him spitting, clearing his throat, squeezing the lemon, answering the call of nature, bathing, observing trivialities, or foolishly laughing. He was very eloquent and well-versed. He did not weep or cry when all his children died. Finally, he used to frequent the princes and men of authority to mediate and think thoroughly and find admonition. So, because of all these he was granted that great wisdom."

Some people claimed that he was offered Prophethood, and that he feared not to be able to carry out its requirements and obligations. Thus, he chose to have wisdom for it is easier this cannot be totally true and Allah knows best! Ikrimah also narrated that Luqman was a Prophet. But this narration is very weak for the sub-narrator, Al-Jafi is mentioned by Imams Al-Bukhari and An-Nasa'i among the Weak Narrators. The majority of scholars are of the view that he was a wise man and not a Prophet. Moreover, he was mentioned in the Glorious Quran and was highly praised by Allah the Almighty Who narrates his advice to his own son in which he says: "O my son! Join not in worship others with Allah. Verily, joining others in worship with Allah is a great Zulm (wrong) indeed," so he forbade his son and warned him against joining others in worship with Allah.

Imam Al-Bukhari said that he was told by Qutaibah after Jarir after Al-Amash after

Ibrahim after Alqamah after Abdullah as saying: 'When the Verse: It is those who believe and do not confuse their belief with wrong (i.e. joining others in worship with Allah) (Al-Anam, 82) was revealed, we said: 'O'Allah's Messenger! Who is there amongst us who has not done wrong to himself?' He (Peace be upon him) replied: "It is not as you say, for 'wrong' in the Verse, do not confuse their belief with wrong means 'SHIRK' (i.e. joining others in worship with Allah). Haven't you heard Luqman's saying to his son, 'O my son! Join not others in worship with Allah, verily joining others in worship with Allah is a great wrong indeed.'" (Luqman, 13)

Allah informs us of His advice to mankind to take care of parents. He states their rights on the children and orders us to be kind with them even if they were polytheists. But, one should not obey them if they invite them to join others in worship *with* Allah. Then Allah resumes Luqman's advice to his son saying: 'O my son! If it be (anything) equal to the weight of a grain of mustard seed, and though it be in a rock, or in the heavens or in the earth, Allah will bring it forth. Verily, Allah is Subtle (in bringing out that grain), Well-Aware (of its place)," i.e. he forbids him to do wrong to the people even in the slightest way, for Allah will bring it forth and bring him to account on the Day of Resurrection. Allah Almighty says: "Surely! Allah wrongs not even of the weight of an atom (or a small ant)." (An-Nisa', 40)

"We shall set up balances of justice on the Day of Resurrection, then none will be dealt with unjustly in anything. And if there be the weight of a mustard seed, We will bring it. And Sufficient are We to take account." (Al-Anbiya', 47)

He told him if that wrong deed was equal to the weight of a grain of mustard seed, or if it was in a solid rock, or in the heavens or in the earth, Allah will bring it forth for He knows its exact place, "Verily, Allah is Subtle (in bringing out that grain), Well-Aware (of its place)."

Allah Almighty also says: "And with Him are the keys of the Ghaib (all that is hidden), none knows them but He. And He knows whatever there is in the land and in the sea; not a leaf falls, but He knows it. There is not a grain in the darkness of the earth nor anything fresh or dry, but is written in a Clear Record."
(Al-An'am, 59)

"There is nothing hidden in the heaven and the earth but it is in a Clear Book (i.e. Al-Lauh Al-Mahfuz)." (An-Naml, 75)
"The All-Knower of the Unseen, it will come to you; not even the weight of an atom (or a small ant) or less than that or greater escapes His Knowledge in the heavens or in the earth but it is in a Clear Book (Al-Lauh Al-Mahfuz)." (Saba, 3).

As-Sadiy claimed that the rock mentioned in the Verse is that which lies beneath the seventh earth. But, this claim is totally rejected for the word "rock" is indefinite and if his claim were true, it would be "the rock". So, "rock" here means any rock whatever and not a particular one.

Narrated Abu Sa'id Al- Khudri after Prophet Muhammad (Peace be upon him) as saying: "If any of you performs deeds in a solid rock that has no door or hole, his deeds, whatever they are, will come out (to the public)."

Luqman said: "O my son! Aqim-As-Salah (perform As-Salah)," i.e. perform the prayer properly and in due time. Then, he said: "enjoin (on people) Al-Maruf (Islamic Monotheism and all that is good), and forbid (people) from Al-Munkar (i.e. disbelief in the Oneness of Allah, polytheists of all kinds and all that is evil and bad)," i.e. with your full power, with your hand, tongue and if you could not, let it be with your heart (i.e. reject and resent it). Then, he advised him to observe patience saying: "and bear with patience whatever befalls you," for if one enjoins what is good and forbids the evil, he will probably regarded as enemy to certain people (but, the final reward would surely be his). For this, he commanded him to observe patience. "These are some of the important commandments (ordered by Allah with no exemption)," that are inevitable and cannot be neglected.

Allah the Almighty said: "And turn not your face away from men with pride," narrated Ibn Abbas, Mujahid, Ikrimah, Sa`id Ibn Jubair, Ad-Dahhak, Yazid Ibn Al-Asam, Abu Al-Jawza and others: This means one should not be showy or arrogant.

Allah the Almighty says: "nor walk in insolence through the earth. Verily, Allah likes not any arrogant boaster," here, Luqman forbids his son to strut in his walk. Allah the Almighty says: "And walk not on the earth with conceit and arrogance. Verily, you can neither rend nor penetrate the earth, nor can you attain a stature like the mountains in height." (Al-Isra, 37) i.e. you will neither be able to tread the whole earth, nor penetrate it with your fast walking or strong footsteps, nor will you be as high as mountains with your showing-off or arrogance. So, know yourself well, for you are only a human being (created to worship Allah Alone).

The Prophetic Hadith states: "While a man was walking, dragging his dress with pride, he was caused to be swallowed by the earth and will go on sinking in it till the Day of Resurrection." (Transmitted by Imam Al-Bukhari in his Sahih)

Another Prophetic Hadith states that: "Beware dragging your dress with pride, for this is boastfulness which is not loved (liked) by Allah. Allah the Almighty said: "Verily, Allah likes not any arrogant boaster."

After Luqman forbids his son to walk boastfully, he orders him to be moderate in his walking, saying: "And be moderate (or show no insolence) in your walking," i.e. do not walk fast or too slow, rather take a course in between, And the (faithful) slaves of the Most Gracious (Allah) are those who walk on the earth in humility and sedateness, and when the foolish address them (with bad words) they reply back with mild words of gentleness. (Al-Furqan, 63) Then, Luqman says: "and lower your voice," i.e. if you talk, do not raise your voice very loudly because the braying of the donkey is the harshest of all voices.

Narrated Abu Hurairah (May Allah be pleased with him): "The Prophet (Peace be upon him) said: 'When you hear the crowing of rooster, ask for Allah's Blessings for (their crowing indicates that) they have seen an angel. And when you hear the braying of donkeys, seek Refuge with Allah from Satan for (their braying indicates) that they have seen a Satan." (Transmitted by Imam Al-Bukhari in his Sahih). For this, it is forbidden to raise one's voice needlessly. But, raising the voice with the Adhan (the Call to Prayer) and in the battlefield is permitted.

These are the pieces of advice given by Luqman to his son that are mentioned in the Glorious Quran. Many others have been mentioned in a book titled Hikmat Luqman (Luqman's Wisdom). From this valuable book, we cite the following: Narrated Imam

Ahmed that Ibn Omar (May Allah be pleased with both of them) said: "We were told by Allah's Messenger (Peace be upon him) that Luqman, the wise used to say: 'If anything was entrusted to Allah, He would preserve it.'"

Narrated Ibn Hatim that Al-Qasim Ibn Mukhaimirah reported that Allah's Messenger (Peace be upon him) said: "Luqman said to his son when he was advising him: "O'my son! Beware of masking for it is treason by night and dispraise during the day."

I was told by my father after Abdah lbn Suleiman after Ibn Al-Mubarak after Abdur Rahman Al-Masudi after Aun Ibn Abdullah as saying: "Luqman said to his son: 'O'my son! If you come to a people's setting, start them with salutation (Saying As-Salamu Alaikum (Peace be with you)), then, take a side and do not utter a word till they speak. If you find them observing the Remembrance of Allah, join them. But, if they observe anything else, turn away from them and seek others (who remember Allah Almighty)."

I was told by my father after Amr Ibn Uthman after Damurah Ibn Hafs Ibn Omar as saying: "Luqman placed a bag of mustards beside him and started to advise his son, giving him with every piece of advice a mustard till it all ran out. He said: "my son! I gave you advice that if a mountain was given, it would split."

Ibn Abbas (May Allah be pleased with him) narrated: "Take care of the black men for three from among them are of the people of Paradise: Luqman the wise, Negus and Bilal (the Caller to Prayer). (However, this Hadith is odd and rejected).

Imam Ahmed, in his book Az-Zuhd (Asceticism), mentioned Luqman's biography and many other valuable things. He said: "I was told by Waki after Sufyan after an unidentified man after Mujahid as saying: Allah's Statement: "And indeed We bestowed upon Luqman Al-Hikmah," i.e. wisdom and religious understanding. He added: "he was not a Prophet." The same was narrated by Wahb Ibn Munabih.

Waki told us after Sufyan after Ash'ath after Ikrimah after Ibn Abbas (May Allah be pleased with him) that he said: "Luqman was an Ethiopian slave."

Aswad told us after Hammad after Ali Ibn Yazid after Sa'id Ibn Al-Musaiyb as saying: "Luqman was a tailor."
Saiyar told us after Ja'far after Malik Ibn Dinar as saying: "Luqman said to his son: 'O'my son! Take Allah's Obedience as your trade, and you will gain profits without having any merchandises.'"

Yazid told us after Abul Ashhab after Muhammad Ibn Wasi as saying: "Luqman said to his son: 'O' my son! Fear Allah and do not let the people notice that you fear Him to gain honor (from them) while your heart is sinful.'"

Yazid Ibn Hamn and Waki told us after Abul Al-Shhab after Khalid Ar-Rab'i as saying: "Luqman was an Ethiopian slave who worked as a carpenter. One day, his master ordered him to slaughter a goat and bring him the most pleasant and delicious two parts thereof. Luqman did so and brought him the tongue and heart. The master asked: Did not you find anything more pleasant than these? Luqman said: No! After a while, the master ordered him to slaughter a goat and to throw the most malignant two parts thereof. Luqman slaughtered the goat and threw the tongue and heart. The master exclaimed and said: I ordered you to bring me the most delicious parts thereof and you brought me the tongue and heart, and I ordered you to throwaway the most malignant parts thereof and you threw the tongue and heart, how can this be?"
Luqman said: "Nothing can be more pleasing than these if they were good, and nothing can be more malicious than these if they were malignant."

Dawud Ibn Rashid told us after Ibn Al-Mubarak after Mu'amir after Abu Uthman, a man from Basrah, as saying: "Luqman said to his son: "O' my son! Do not wish for befriending a fool that he may think you approve his foolishness. And, do not take the wise man's rage easily that he may abstain from you."

Dawud Ibn Usaid told us after Ismail Ibn Ayyash after Damdam Ibn Zar'ah after Shuraih Ibn Ubaid Al-Hadrami after Abdullah Ibn Zaid as saying: "Luqman said: 'Verily, Allah's Hand is on the mouths of wise men; none of them speaks but with what Allah assigned for him.'"

Abdur Razzaq told us that he heard Ibn Juraij as saying: "I used to mask my head at night and Omar said to me: Luqman had said: 'masking during the day is humiliation and at night is dispraise.' So, why do you mask yourself at night? He said: Luqman was not indebted."

I was told by Hasan after Al-Junaid after Sufyan as saying: Luqman said to his son: "O' my son! I have never regretted because of keeping silent. If words are silver, silence is golden."
I was told by Abdul Samad and Waki after Abul Ashhab after Qatadah as saying: "Luqman said to his son: 'O' my son! Set apart with evil and it will set apart with you, for evil begets nothing but evil.'"

Narrated Imam Ahmed: "I was told by Abdur Rahman Ibn Mahdi after Nafi' Ibn Omar after Ibn Abu Malikah after Ubaid Ibn Omair as saying: Luqman said to his son when he was advising him: 'O'my son! Choose between gatherings (of people) precisely! If you find a gathering in which Allah is mentioned, sit yourself with them. Thus, if you are knowledgeable, your knowledge will benefit you; but, if you are ignorant, they will teach you; and if Allah wishes to do them good, you will be benefited therewith. O'my son! Do not sit in a gathering in which Allah is not mentioned! Because if you are knowledgeable, your knowledge will not benefit you; and if you are ignorant, they will add to your ignorance; and if Allah wishes to afflict them with harm, you will be afflicted with them. O'my son! Do not rejoice at seeing a strong man who sheds the blood of the faithful, for Allah appoints for him a killer that does not ever die.'"

Abu Mu'awiyah told us after Hisham Ibn Urwah after his father as saying: Wisdom dictates: "O'my son: Let your speech be good and your face be smiling, you will be more loved by the people than those who give them provisions." And, he said: "It is stated in the wisdom -or the Torah. Kindness is the head of wisdom." And, he said: "It is stated in the Torah. As you show mercy (to others), mercy will be shown to you." And, he said: "It is stated in the wisdom: You will gain what you give (or, harvest what you grow)." And, he said: "It is stated in the wisdom: "Love your friend and the friend of your father."

Abdur Razzaq told us after Mu'amir after Ayyub after Abu Qulabah as saying: Luqman was once asked: "Who is the best one in terms of patience?" He said: "It is the one who practices no harm after observing patience." Those who asked him said: "Who is the best one in terms of knowledge?" He said: "It is he who adds to his own knowledge through the knowledge of others." They asked: "Who is the best from among the whole people?" He said: "It is the wealthy." They said: "Is it the one who has properties and riches?" He said: "No! But, it is the one if whose good was sought, he would not hold it back or prevent it. And, it is the one who does not need anything from others."

Narrated Sufyan Ibn Uyaynah: Luqman was asked: "Who is the worst of all people?" He replied: "It is the one who does not feel shame if found committing a sinful deed."

Abu As-Samad told us after Malik Ibn Dianr as saying: I found some pieces of wisdom as follows: "Allah Almighty scatters and wastes the bones of those who give religious opinions that go with the people's lusts and desires." "There is no good for you that you learn something new while you do not practice what you have learnt previously. This is like a man who gathered a pile of dry wood, then tried to carry it but couldn't. Thereupon, he collected a second one."

Abdullah Ibn Ahmed said: I was told by Al-Hakam Ibn Abu Zuhair Ibn Musa after Al-Faraj Ibn Fudalah after Abu Sa'id as saying: Luqman said to his son: "O'my son! Let only the pious men eat your food, and consult the scholars over your affairs." These were what Imam Ahmed quoted from the wisdom of Luqman, and I added some that he did not transmit and indeed, he Imam Ahmed quoted things that I did not. And, Allah knows best!

Ibn Abu Hatim said: I was told by my father after Al-Abbas Ibn Al-Walid after Zaid Ibn Yahya Ibn Ubaid Al-Khuza'i after Sa'id Ibn Bashir after Qatadah as saying: "Allah Almighty enabled Luqman to choose between Prophethood and wisdom and he (Luqman) preferred wisdom to Prophethood. Then, Gabriel came while he was asleep and poured the wisdom over him. And, he began to pronounce it the next morning."

Sa'id said: I heard Qatadah as saying: It was said to Luqman: "How did you prefer wisdom to Prophethood when you were enabled to choose between them?" He said: "If Allah were to assign me with Prophethood, I would accept it and try hard to win His Pleasure, but He enabled me to choose. I feared of being too weak for Prophethood, so I chose wisdom."

This narration is not perfectly authentic or sound for that sub-narrator. Sa'id Ibn Bashir, is not a trustworthy one. However, many from among our earlier scholars, foremost among whom were: Mujahid, Sa'id Ibn Al-Musayyb and Ibn Abbas (May Allah be pleased with him) were of the viewpoint that Allah's Statement that reads: "And indeed We bestowed upon Luqman Al-Hikmah (wisdom)," means: discretion and religious understanding. Thereupon, he was not a Prophet and nothing has been revealed to him Al-Wahi (Divine Inspiration).

The Story of People of the Ditch (17)

Allah the Almighty said:

"By the heaven holding the big stars. And by the Promised Day (i.e. the Day of Resurrection). And by the Witnessing day (i.e. Friday), and by the Witnessed day (i.e. the Day of Arafat (Hajj), the ninth of Dhul-Hijjah). Cursed were the people of the Ditch (in the story of the Boy and the King). Of fire fed with fuel. When they sat by it (fire). And they witnessed what they were doing against the believers (i.e. burning them). And they had no fault except that they believed in Allah, the All-Mighty, Worthy of all Praise! To Whom belongs the dominion of the heavens and the earth! And Allah is Witness over everything. Verily, those who put into trial the believing men and believing women (by torturing them and burning them), and then do not turn in repentance (to Allah), then they will have the torment of Hell, and they will have the punishment of the burning Fire." (Al-Buruj, 1-10)

Muhammad Ibn Ishaq claimed that they lived after the advent of Jesus (Peace be upon him), but other scholars disagreed with him claiming them to live before him (Peace be upon him). However, many scholars mentioned that this incident was repeated more than once.

Allah's Messenger (Peace be upon him) said: "There lived a king before you and he had a (court) magician. As he (the magician) grew old, he said to the king: I have grown old, send some young boy to me so that I should teach him magic. He (the king) sent him a young boy so that he should train him (in magic). And on his way (to the magician) he (the young boy) found a monk sitting there. He listened to the monk's and was impressed by it. It became his habit to pass by the monk and spent the time with him listening to his teachings and then leave to the magician late. He (the magician) beat him because of delay. He made a complaint of that to the monk and he said to him: When you feel afraid of the magician, say: Members of my family had detained me. And when you feel afraid of your family you should say: The magician had detained me. It so happened that there came a huge beast (of prey) and it blocked the way of the people, and he (the young boy) said: I will, come to know today whether the magician is superior or the monk is superior. He picked up a stone and said: 'OAllah, if the affair of the monk is dearer to Thee than the affair of the magician, cause death to this animal so that the people should be able to move about freely.' He threw that stone towards it and killed it and the people began to move about (on the path freely).

He (the young man) then came to that monk and informed him and the monk said: 'Today you are superior to me. Your affair has come to a stage where I find that you would be soon put to a trial, and in case you are put to a trial do not give my clue. That young man began to treat the blind and those suffering from leprosy. He in fact began to cure people from (all kinds) of illness. When a companion of the king who had gone blind heard about him, he came to him with numerous gifts and said: "if you cure me, all these things collected together here would be yours.'

He said: "I myself do not cure anyone. It is Allah Who cures and if you affirm faith in Allah, I shall also supplicate Allah to cure you." He affirmed his faith in Allah and Allah cured him and he came to the king and sat by his side as he used to sit before. The king said to him: "Who restored your eyesight?" He said: "My Lord!" The king got astounded: "Should it mean that your Lord is another One besides me." He said: "My Lord and your Lord is Allah," so he (the king) took hold of him and tormented him until he gave a clue of that boy. The young man was thus summoned and the king said to him: "O'boy, it has been conveyed to me that you have become so much proficient in your magic that you cure the blind and those suffering from leprosy and you do such and such things." The boy said: "I do not cure anyone; it is Allah Who cures." The king took hold of him and began to torment him. Eventually the boy gave a clue of the monk. The monk was thus summoned and it was said to him: "You should turn back from your religion. He, however, refused to do so." He (ordered) for a saw to be brought (and when it was done) he (the king) placed it in the middle of his head and tore it into parts till a part fell down. Then the courtier of the king was brought and it was said to him: "Turn back from your religion. And he refused to do so, and the saw was placed in the midst of his head and it was torn till a part fell down."

Then that young boy was brought and it was said to him: "Turn back from your religion." He refused to do so and he was handed over to a group of his courtiers.

The king ruled: "Take him to such and such mountain, and make him climb up that mountain and when you reach its top (ask him to renounce his faith) but if he refuses to do so, then throw him (down the mountain)." So they took him and made him climb up the mountain and he said: "O'Allah, save me from them (in any way)."

The mountain began to quake and they all fell down and he came walking to the king. The king said to him: "What has happened to your companions (the courtiers)? He said: "Allah has saved me from them."

He again handed him to some of his courtiers and said: "Take him and carry him in a small boat and when you reach the middle of the ocean (ask him to renounce) his religion, but if he does not renounce his religion throw him (into the water)." So they took him and the boy said: "O'Allah, save me from them and what they want to do." At that moment, the boat turned over and they were drowned and he came walking to the king, and the king said to him: "What has happened to your companions (the courtiers)? He said: "Allah has saved me from them, and he said to the king: You cannot kill me until you do what I ask you to do."

And he said: What is that? He said: "You should gather people in a plain and hang me by the trunk (of a tree). Then take hold of an arrow from the quiver and say: 'In the name of Allah, the Lord of the worlds,' then shoot an arrow and if you do that then you would be able to kill me."
The king called the people in an open plain and tied the boy to the trunk of a tree,

then he took hold of an arrow from his quiver and then placed the arrow in the bow and then said: "In the Name of Allah, the Lord of the young boy." He then shot an arrow and it bit his temple. He (the boy) placed his hands upon the temple where the arrow had bit him and he died and the people said: "We affirm our faith in the Lord of this young man, we affirm our faith in the Lord of this young man, and we affirm our faith in the Lord of this young man."

The courtiers came to the king and it was said to him: "Do you see that Allah has actually done what you aimed at averting. They (the people) have affirmed their faith in the Lord." The king commanded ditches to be dug at certain points in the path. When these ditches were dug, and the fire was lit in them it was said (to the people): "He who would not turn back from his (the boy's) religion would be thrown in the fire or it would be said to them to jump in it." (The people courted death but did not renounce religion) until a woman came with her child and she felt hesitant in jumping into the fire and the child said to her: "O'mother, endure (this ordeal) for it is the Truth." (Transmitted by Imam Ahmed, Imam Muslim and An-Nasa'i from the Hadith of Hammad Ibn Salamah).

Some scholars claimed that the incident of the ditch was recurred or repeated in the past more than once. Ibn Abu Hatim said: "I was told by my father after Abul Yaman after Safwan Ibn Abdur Rahman Ibn Jubair as saying: The incident of the ditch took place in the Yemen during the lifetime of Tubba. And, it took place in Constantinople during the lifetime of Constantine who set the fires in which he threw the Christians who were sticking to the religion of Jesus (Islamic Monotheism). It also took place in Iraq, in the land of Babylon during the lifetime of Bikhtinassar who erected an idol and ordered the people to prostrate themselves before it. Daniel, Izrya and Mashayl refused and thereupon, he set a great fire and threw them into it. However, Allah Almighty saved them from the fire and caused the 9 men who transgressed over them to fell into the fire they themselves made.

Concerning Allah's Statement that reads: "Cursed were the people of the Ditch," As-Sadiy said: "There were three ditches: one in Sham (Syria), another in Iraq, and the third in the Yemen." (Narrated by Ibn Abu Hatim)

The Story of Barsisa the Worshipper (The Renegade) (18)

Allah the Almighty said in His Glorious Quran:

"Their allies deceived them like Shaitan (Satan), when he says to man: 'Disbelieve in Allah.' But when (man) disbelieves in Allah, Shaitan (Satan) says: 'I am free of you, I fear Allah, the Lord of the Alamin (mankind, jinn and all that exists)!' So the end of both will be that they will be in the Fire, abiding therein. Such is the recompense of the Zalimun (i.e. polytheists, wrongdoers, disbelievers in Allah and in His Oneness)." (Al-Hashr, 16, 17)

Ibn Jarir said that Abdullah Ibn Masud interpreted the Quranic Verse that reads: (Their allies deceived them) like Shaitan (Satan), when he says to man: 'Disbelieve in Allah.' But when (man) disbelieves in Allah, Shaitan (Satan) says: "I am free of you, I fear Allah, the Lord of the Alamin (mankind, jinn and all that exists)!" So the end of both will be that they will be in the Fire, abiding therein. Such is the recompense of the Zalimun (i.e. polytheists, wrong-doers, disbelievers in Allah and in His Oneness). (Al-Hashr, 16, 17)

Ibn Masud (May Allah be pleased with him) said: "Once upon a time, there was a woman grazing sheep and goats. She had 4 brothers. She (for some reason) used to spend the night at a monk's cell. The monk committed adultery with her and she got pregnant. Satan came to him and said: "Kill the woman and then bury her for you are a reputable and highly respected man (i.e. don't risk your own reputation for such a simple woman). "

The monk killed her and then buried her. Thereupon, Satan visited her 4 brothers in a dream while they were asleep and said to them: "the monk committed adultery with your sister, and because she got pregnant, he killed her and buried her in such-and-such location."

In the morning, one of them said: "By Allah! Last night I dreamt of something and I do not know whether to relate it to you or just keep it to myself?" They said: Relate it to us. He did so and one of them said: "By Allah! I saw the same dream. Another said the same. And the fourth one said the same thing. They agreed on that there must be something serious about that dream."

They went to the king and appealed for his help against the monk. The king's troops came to arrest him and he was taken away. On the way, Satan came to the monk (and whispered in his ears): "No one can save you from the king. Prostrate yourself before me just for once and I will save you from this. Thereupon, the monk prostrated himself before Satan. When they presented themselves before the king, Satan said to him: "I am free of you!" Finally, the monk was killed.

The same story was narrated by the Leader of the Believers, Ali Ibn Abu Talib (May Allah be pleased with him) in another wording. Ibn Jarir said: I was told by Khallad Ibn Aslam, on the authority of An-Nadr Ibn Shamil after Shu'bah, after Abu Ishaq, after 'Abdullah Ibn Nahik saying: "I heard Ali as saying: A monk worshipped Allah Alone for 60 years. Satan exerted himself to seduce him, but could not. He went to a woman and touched her with evil (maddened her). The woman had brothers whom were visited by Satan who told them to take her to that monk to receive treatment and cure. They took her to the monk and he treated her. Afterwards, she stayed for a while at his cell (house). One day, he was attracted to her and he committed adultery with her. She got pregnant and he killed her (to conceal his first crime). Her brothers came (after knowing the matter) and Satan appeared again for the monk and said: I am your friend, I did not find a solution or way to mislead you. Obey me and I will save you from this. Prostrate yourself before me and you will be saved. The monk did so. Then, Satan said: I am free of you, I fear Allah, the Lord of the Alamin (mankind, jinn and all that exists)!
(Al- Hashr ,16)

Allah said: "Their allies deceived them like Shaitan (Satan), when he says to man: Disbelieve in Allah. But when (man) disbelieves in Allah, Shaitan (Satan) says: I am free of you, I fear Allah, the Lord of the Alamin (mankind, jinn and all that exists)! So the end of both will be that they will be in the Fire, abiding therein. Such is the recompense of the Zalimun (i.e. polytheists, wrong-doers, disbelievers in Allah and in His Oneness)." (Al-Hashr, 16, 17)

The Story of Yemen and Owners of the Elephant (19)

Allah the Almighty said:

Have you O'Muhammad (peace and blessings be upon him) not seen how your Lord dealt with the owners of the Elephant? [The Elephant army which came from Yemen under the command of Abraha Al-Ashram intending to destroy the Kabbah at Makkah]. Did He not make their plot go astray? And He sent against them birds, in flocks. Striking them with stones of Sijjil (baked clay). And He made them like (an empty field on stalks (of which the corn has been eaten up by cattle)."
(Al-Phil, 1-5)

At Tabari said: "The first one to tame elephants was Ifridun Ibn Athqiyan who killed Ad-Dahhaq. He was the first to use saddle for horses. But, the first one to tame and ride on horses was Tahmuris, the third king on earth. It is also said that Ismail Ibn Ibrahim (Peace be upon them) was the first to ride horses. It is probably that he was the first one to ride on them from among the Arabs, and Allah knows the best."

It is said: "Though the elephant is so huge, he fears from cats. Thereupon, some warlords, during their fight against the Indians, brought some cats to the battlefield the matter that forced the elephants to bolt."

Ibn Ishaq said: "The governor or viceroy, Abraha Al-Ashram built a huge and very lofty church, and wrote to the king of Abyssinia, Negus that he have built him a church that is unprecedented, and he is intending to divert pilgrimage from Mecca to Abyssinia."
Al-Suhaili said: Abraha Al-Ashram subjugated the Yemenites to build that church

and forced them to taste several sorts of humiliation. He used to cut off the hand of the one who comes late for labor until the sun rises. He took many valuable things from the palace of Bilqis to add thereto. He took marbles, precious stones, and valuable luggage. Moreover, he erected gold and silver crosses, built ebony and ivory pulpits, and raised the church's stature and expanded its width. Afterwards, when Abraha was killed, whosoever tried to take anything out of its body or ornaments, the Jinn were reluctant and hesitant to do him harm. For, it was built above the burial of two idols called Kuaib and his wife, the height of which was about 60 cubits. So, the Yemenites left it untouched until the era of Al-Saffah, the first Abbaside Caliph.

Ibn Ishaq said: When the Arabs heard of the letter of Abraha sent to Negus, a man from Kinanah got angry. He set out till he reached the church where he urinated on its walls. Nobody noticed him, and upon that he returned home safely. The news reached Abraha who asked about the doer. He was answered: this was done by one of those Arabs who perform pilgrimage to the Kabbah at Mecca when he heard of your declared intention that you would divert pilgrimage from their Sacred House to your (recently-built) church. He (the Arab) got angry and came to excrete therein declaring it to be unqualified (to the event). Upon hearing this, Abraha burst with rage and took oath that he would demolish the Kabbah. Then, he ordered the Abyssinians (Christians) to get prepared for war. He led a big expedition against Mecca accompanying an elephant or elephants in his train.

The Arabs heard of the news and they were terrified, but they decided to fight him when the news was affirmed that he intended to destroy the Sacred House. A man from among the noblemen of Yemen called Dhu Nafar set out for him accompanied with his own clan and those who answered his call to fight against Abraha. The two parties met, Dhu Nafar and his followers were defeated and he himself was taken as a prisoner of war. He was then brought before Abraha who was about to kill him, but Dhu Nafar said: "O'king! Do not kill me, I may be of any use to you."

Abraha did not kill him and he kept him tied up in custody. Then Abraha went on intending what he set out for. He arrived at the land of Khatham where he encountered with Nufail Ibn Habib Al-Khathami who was leading his two tribes: Shahran and Nahis, along with his followers from among the Arabs. Nufail was defeated and taken as a prisoner of war to be brought before Abraha. Abraha intended to kill him, but Nufail said: "O'king! Do not kill me. I may guide you to the destination you desire. Here you are! My pledge of allegiance.
Abraha set him free and took him as a guide. When they passed by Ta'if, there came to him Masud Ibn Mutab Ibn Malik Ibn Kab Ibn Amr Ibn Sa'd Ibn Auf Ibn Thaqif

along with his followers who said: "O'king! We are nothing but your slaves, we listen and obey, no hostility is ever there between you and us, and our House is not that which you want, i.e. Al-Lat, but you want the House in Mecca. Hence, we send with you someone who leads you thereto.

Ibn Ishaq said: Al-Lat was a 'sacred' House in Ta'if, it was to them just as the Kabbah was to the rest of the Arabs. They sent a man called Abu Rughal to show him (Abraha) the way to Mecca. They went on till they arrived at a place called Al-Maghmas where Abu Rughal died. Abu Rughal was buried there and afterwards, the Arabs used to stone his grave.

However, I mentioned on the Story of Thamud that Abu Rughal was among the train of Abraha and that he sheltered himself with the Sacred House (Kabbah) and when he came out, a stone hit him and he was dead. The Prophet (Peace be upon him) told his Companions: "As a sign on this, he was buried with two branches of gold." They dug and verily, they found them. To compromise between this and the narration of Ibn Ishaq: the later Abu Rughal had the same name as his higher ancestor whose grave used to be stoned by the Arabs. Moreover, the people used to stone his grave as they stone that of the former.

Ibn Ishaq said: When Abraha arrived at Al-Maghmas, he sent a man called Al-Aswad Ibn Maqsud with a cavalry dispatch. Al-Aswad seized some of the Arab's property which included two hundred camels that belonged to Abdul Muttalib, the Prophet's uncle, who was, then, the principal man among the nobility.

Upon this, Quraish, Kinanah and Hudhail decided to fight against Abraha, but they comprehended that they cannot afford that and thus quitted the idea. Then, Abraha sent Hanatah Al-Himiari to Mecca ordering him to ask about the chief of the people and tell him: "I (the king) did not come to fight against you, 1 only came to destroy the Sacred House. If you do not stand in our way, we will not harm any of you all."

Abraha added to his messenger: "And if he showed his desire not to fight, bring him to me." When Hanatah entered Mecca, he asked about its chief and master. He was told: it is Abdul Muttalib Ibn Hashim. He saw him and thus delivered the message. Abdul Muttalib said: "By Allah! We do not intend to fight. Really we cannot afford it. This is the Sacred House of Allah and His Khalil (friend) Ibrahim (Peace be upon him), only Him Alone can protect it if He wills to."
Upon hearing this, Hanatah said: "Come with me to meet with him (Abraha), he ordered me to do so." Abdul Muttalib set out for him accompanied with some of his sons till they approached the camp. He asked about Dhu Nafar who was a friend of

his. He entered upon him in his prison and said: "O'Dhu Nafar! Can't you do anything for us in this plight of ours?"

Abdul Muttalib, the grandfather of the Holy Prophet Muhammad (s.a.w.), went to meet Abraha because he wanted his camels back. Abraha expressed his surprise that Abdul Muttalib never asked anything about the Kaaba. In response, he told him that the owner of the Kaabah would take care of His house.

Dhu Nafar said: "What can a prisoner do while waiting for death to come either in the morning of at night? All that 1 can do is to send to the stableman of the elephant, Anis, who is a friend of mine to recommend you, say a good word of you, intercede for you before him, and to seek permission for you to meet with Abraha."

Abdul Muttalib said: "That's enough with me." Dhu Nafar sent to Anis saying: Verily, Abdul Muttalib is the chief of the Quraishites, he is generous to both humans and animals and the king (Abraha) seized two hundred camels that belong to him. So, seek permission for him to meet Abraha and do whatever you see useful for him."

Anis said: "I will do." Anis presented himself before Abraha and then said: "O'king! The chief of Quraish is here and wants to present himself before you, so give him permission to, please!"

Abraha gave his consent. Abdul Muttalib was very handsome and grand and when seen by Abraha, Abraha showed great respect and was highly impressed. So, he refused to make him sit lowly in front of him, and also disliked to let the Abyssinians see him allowing him to sit on his own chair (throne).
Consequently, he descended from above his chair and sat beside him on the rich carpet. Then, he said to his interpreter: "Ask him what he wants?" However, Abraha was surprised to hear from Abdul Muttalib through the interpreter that all he wanted was a compensation for his two hundred camels, but did not ask him to leave the

Kabbah alone.

When Abraha expressed surprise, Abdul Muttalib answered: "I am the master of the camels, whereas the Kabbah house of worship. It has its lord to defend it."

Abraha said: No one can defend it from me. Abdul Muttalib said: "You are on your own!" Finally, Abraha gave him the camel's back.

Ibn Ishaq said: "It is said that when Abdul Muttalib entered upon Abraha he was accompanied with Ya'mur Ibn Nafa'ah Ibn Adiy Ibn Ad-Dail Ibn Bakr Ibn Abd Manah Ibn Kinanah the chief of the Banu Bakr tribe and Khuwailid Ibn Wa'ilah the chief of the Hudhail tribe who offered Abraha one-third of the properties of Tihamah district in return for his going back and leaving the Kabbah alone. But, Abraha refused their offer. However, Ibn Ishaq added: "I am not certain about the authenticity of this!"

When Abdul Muttalib returned home he told the Quraishites about what happened between him and Abraha and ordered them to evacuate Mecca and move to the mountains. Then, he accompanied with some men stood holding the ring of the Kabah's door invoking Allah and seeking His Aid against Abraha and his troops.

Ibn Ishaq said: "Abdul Muttalib let the door's ring and set out with his companions to the mountains seeking shelter and awaiting for what would happen next. In the morning, Abraha got prepared to enter Mecca, and got his elephant and troops prepared. The elephant's name was Mahmoud. When he was directed towards Mecca, Nufail Ibn Habib came near him and whispered in his ear: "Kneel down Mahmoud and go back home safe, you are in Allah's Sacred Town." He let go his ear and the elephant kneeled down.

As-Suhaili said: this means that the elephant fell to the ground, as elephants do not kneel down. It is said: that some elephants might kneel down just as camels. And, Allah Knows Best.

Nufail Ibn Habib went away and climbed up the mount until he was far and safe.

The Abyssinians beat the elephant forcing him to stand up to his feet, but he refused. They hit his head with axe-like weapons, but he refused. They tried their best to force him to stand up to his feet, but they could not. They directed his face back towards the Yemen and he stood up and ran thereto. They directed him towards the

Sham (Syria) and then towards the east and he stood up to his feet and ran thereto. They again directed him towards Mecca, but he refused. Thereupon, Allah the Almighty sent upon them birds from the seaside resembling hawks. Each bird held 3 stones: one in his beak and two in his two legs. The stones were like chick-peas and lentils, and none from among the Abyssinians was hit by a stone, but he was killed. Moreover, the birds did not hit them all. The rest of them fled away seeking the way they first came from and asking about Nufail Ibn Habib to guide them back to Yemen.

Just before the final attack, the biggest elephant would not move any further, even though they tried very hard to push it.

Ibn Ishaq said: the Abyssinians fled away while death pursuing them on every path and in every way and Abraha was hit with a stone as well. They carried him and his body began to tear up part after part till they reached San'aa. After a short while, his chest cracked (as claimed by historians) and he died.

Ibn Ishaq said: I have been told by Ya'qub Ibn Utbah that that year was the first in which measles, small-box, and bitter trees such as colocynth and African rue appeared in the Arab Peninsula.

Ibn Ishaq said: When Allah the Almighty sent His Prophet Muhammad (peace and blessings be upon him), He reminded the Quraishites with His Grace and Favor bestowed on them through defeating the Abyssinians and defying them saying: "Have you O'Muhammad (peace be upon him) not seen how your Lord dealt with the owners of the Elephant?"
Did He not make their plot go astray? And He sent against them birds, (Ababil) in flocks. Striking them with stones of Sijjil (baked clay). And He made them like (an empty field of) stalks (of which the corn has been eaten up by cattle)."

Then, Ibn Hisham and Ibn Ishaq started to interpret this Surah and the next stated as follows: Ibn Hisham said: The word 'Ababil' means "in flocks", though the Arabs never used that word before the Revelation of the Glorious Quran.

But as for the word "Sijjil", I was told by Yunus An-Nahwi and Abu' Ubaidah that it was used by the Arabs to mean: solid and strong. Moreover, some interpreters claimed that this word was originally two in Persian, but the Arabs rendered them a single word that is "Sinj" and "lil". 'Sinj' means stone and lil' stands for clay and hard stones consist of these two materials, stone and clay. He added, "Assf" stands for leaves. Al-Kasa'i said: I have heard some grammarians saying: "The singular form of 'Ababil' (flock) is 'Abil'. Besides, many of our early scholars said: 'Ababil' are flocks of birds gathering group after group from here and there.

Narrated Abdullah Ibn Abbas (May Allah be pleased with them): Their beaks were like those of the birds and their legs were like those of the dogs. In addition, Ikrimah transmitted: their heads were like those of the lions and they came from the seaside and their color was green. Also, Ubaid Ibn Omair said: they were marine black birds, holding stones in their beaks and legs. Abdullah Ibn Abbas (May Allah be pleased with him) said also: they looked like the Phoenix, and the smallest stone they carried was equal to the head of a human being and other stones were equal to camels. The same view was held by Yunus Ibn Bakir after Ibn Ishaq. Some interpreters said: The stones were too small. Allah knows best!

Ibn Abu Hatim said: Abu Zarah told us on the authority of Muhammad Ibn Abdullah Ibn Abu Shaibah after Mu'awiyah after Al-Amash after Abu Sufyan after Ubaid Ibn Omair saying: When Allah the Almighty wanted to destroy the owners of the elephant He sent against them birds in flocks from the seaside resembling hawks, each one of them carried three stones: one in his beak and two in his two legs. They flew over till they were directly above the army, then they screamed and let go of the stones.

The stones used to cut off or crack whom they hit from his head to his toes. In addition, Allah the Almighty sent a severe wind that hit the stones and added to their speed and strength, the matter that caused the majority of the army to perish.

Ibn Ishaq said as stated earlier that not all of them were hit by the stones. Rather, some of them managed to return to the Yemen and related to their people what had happened to them and to the whole army. And Abraha himself was hit with the stones and was carried until he reached the Yemen where he died.

Narrated Ibn Ishaq saying: I was told by Abdullah Ibn Abu Bakr after Samurah after Aishah (May Allah be pleased with her) that she said: "I have seen the rider and stableman of the elephant at Mecca blind, crippled and asking the people to feed them up." However, it was mentioned earlier that the stableman was called Anis, but the rider was unidentified. Allah knows best!

In his Tafsir (interpretation), An-Naqqash mentioned that the flood carried away their dead bodies and threw them into the sea. At the same year of this great incident, Prophet Muhammad (peace and blessings be upon him) was born. Some scholars say that it took place two years prior to his (peace be upon him) birth.

Then, Ibn Ishaq cited the poetry the Arabs composed pertaining to that great incident in which Allah the Almighty made victorious His Sacred House which He wanted to grant honor, dignity, purification and respect through sending His Messenger Muhammad (peace and blessings be upon him) and the Legislation He sends with him. One of the fundamental pillars of this Legislation is the Prayer whose Qiblah direction would be made to the honorable Kabbah. That which Allah the Almighty did to the owners of the elephant was never for the sake of the Quraishites themselves. As the Christians who were represented in the Abyssinians were really nearer to the Kabbah than the polytheists of Quraish, but the victory was granted to the Sacred House itself in preparation for the advent of Prophet Muhammad (peace and blessings be upon him).

Added Ibn Ishaq and others: After the death of Abraha, the Abyssinians were ruled by his son, Yaksum, then by his brother, Masruq Ibn Abraha who was their last king.

The incident of the elephant took place in Al-Muharram, 882 according to the Roman calendar. Following the death of Abraha and his succeeding two sons, the Abyssinian rule over the Yemen came to an end, the church built by Abraha was deserted.

No one could even approach the church for it was built over the burial place of two idols that of Ku'aib and his wife. The two idols were made of wood, their height was about 60 cubits and they were touched with the jinn. For this very reason, no one could take the risk to come near the church or to take anything of its building or ornaments fearing the evils of the jinn. It stayed deserted until the time of the first

Abbaside Caliph, As-Saffah whom the news of the riches found inside the church reached. He sent his ruler over the Yemen, Al-Abbas Ibn Ar-Rabi to destroy it and bring him all the precious objects he might find there.

Finally, one should raise his hands to Allah the Almighty and supplicate:

"O'Allah! All the Praises are for You. You are the Light of the Heavens and the Earth. And all the Praises are for You. You are the Keeper of the Heavens and the Earth. All the Praises are for You. You are the Lord of the Heavens and the Earth and whatever is therein. You are the Truth, and Your Promise is the Truth, and Your Speech is the Truth, and meeting You is the Truth, and Paradise is the Truth and Hell (Fire) is the Truth and all the prophets are the Truth and the Hour is the Truth. O'Allah! I surrender to You, and I believe in You, and depend upon You, and repent to You, and in Your cause I fight and with Your orders I rule. So please forgive my past and future sins and those sins which I did in secret or in public. It is You Whom I worship, none has the right to be worshipped except You."

www.ingramcontent.com/pod-product-compliance
Lightning Source LLC
Chambersburg PA
CBHW071856070526
44583CB00016B/1720